The
Year
of the
Poet XI

July 2024

The Poetry Posse

inner child press, ltd.

'building bridges of cultural understanding'

The Poetry Posse 2024

Gail Weston Shazor
Shareef Abdur Rasheed
Teresa E. Gallion
hülya n. yılmaz
Noreen Snyder
Tzemin Ition Tsai
Elizabeth Esguerra Castillo
Jackie Davis Allen
Mutawaf Shaheed
Caroline 'Ceri' Nazareno
Ashok K. Bhargava
Alicja Maria Kuberska
Swapna Behera
Albert 'Infinite' Carrasco
Michelle Joan Barulich
Eliza Segiet
William S. Peters, Sr.

~ * ~

In order to maintain each poet's authentic voice, this volume has not undergone the scrutiny of editing. Please take time to indulge each contributor for their own creativity and aspirations to convey their uniqueness.

hülya n. yılmaz, Ph.D.
Director of Editing ~
Inner Child Press International

The Year of the Poet XI
July 2024 Edition

The Poetry Posse

1st Edition : 2024

Publisher Information
1st Edition : Inner Child Press
intouch@innerchildpress.com
www.innerchildpress.com

Copyright © 2024 : The Poetry Posse

ISBN-13 : 978-1-961498-32-7 (inner child press, ltd.)

$ 12.99

WHAT WOULD LIFE BE WITHOUT A LITTLE POETRY?

$\mathcal{D}$edication

This Book is dedicated to

Humanity, Peace & Poetry

the Power of the Pen

can effectuate change!

&

The Poetry Posse

past, present & future,

our Patrons and Readers &

the Spirit of our Everlasting Muse

In the darkness of my life
I heard the music
I danced . . .
and the Light appeared
and I dance

Janet P. Caldwell

Table of Contents

The Poetry Posse

Table of Contents . . . *continued*

July's Featured Poets   119

Inner Child Press News   151

Other Anthological Works   191

Foreword
Renowned Poets
Pablo Neruda

(1904-1973)

The Poetry Posse Family has another powerful motivating factor for writers and poets worldwide with this July issue. This compendium is a testament to Pablo Neruda's evocative poetry, passionate verses, and unwavering commitment to social justice.

Born Neftalí Ricardo Reyes Basoalto on July 12, 1904, in Parral, Chile, and passing away on September 23, 1973, in Santiago, Pablo Neruda was a remarkable Chilean poet, diplomat, and politician. His literary legacy extends far beyond his native country, making him one of the most influential Latin American poets of the 20th century.

Neruda left an indelible mark on world literature. His influence extends far beyond his native land, resonating with readers across borders and languages. The impacts of his writings earned global recognition and transcended borders. Despite being relatively unknown to North Americans, Neruda is one of the most influential 20th-century poets in the Americas.

Neruda's poetic journey began early; he wrote his first poems at the tender age of 10. Neruda's vivid imagery transports us to the ancient Inca city, where he contemplates the human condition and the weight of time. Neruda's frank, cosmic portrayal of love, and commitment to communism resonated deeply with readers, making him a unique voice in the literary landscape.

His most widely read collection,Veinte Poemas de Amor y una Canción Desesperada (Twenty Love Poems and a Song of Despair) (1924), emerged from the depths of an unhappy love affair. This cycle of love poems, published when Neruda was still young, catapulted him into prominence. It celebrated both sensuality and displacement, intertwining memories of love affairs with the wilderness of southern Chile.

"Tonight I Can Write (The Saddest Lines)"In this poignant poem, Neruda reflects on lost love, longing, and the vastness of the night sky. 'If You Forget Me', is another free-verse lyric that calls for mutual forgetting and mutual memory. The melancholic verses capture the ache of absence and the beauty of memory. "Canto XII from The Heights of Macchu Picchu" is an epic poem that explores themes of history, identity, and human struggle. In 1971, Neruda received the Nobel Prize in Literature, a decision that sparked controversy but solidified his place as one of the greatest Spanish-language poets of all time. His impact on literature and culture remains enduring, corroboration of his eloquence, creativity, and unwavering dedication to the written word.

His celebration of human emotions, explicit yet universal, continues to resonate with readers today. His legacy reminds us of the enduring power of language and poetry.
Pablo Neruda's writings remain timeless classics, touching hearts and minds across cultures. His

poetic journey, from the backwoods of southern Chile to global acclaim, enriches our understanding of love, nature, and the human experience.

Let's enjoy and feel the fire in these readings, as Neruda wrote "To feel the love of people whom we love is a fire that feeds our life."

Caroline Nazareno-Gabis

Selected E-sources:

https://www.poetryfoundation.org/poets/pablo-neruda
https://nationalopedia.com/chile-national-poet-pablo-neruda/

Selected Poems of Pablo Neruda (pablonerudafilm.com)
Titles and themes of Pablo Neruda's poems
Britannica.com
Wikipedia

Now Available

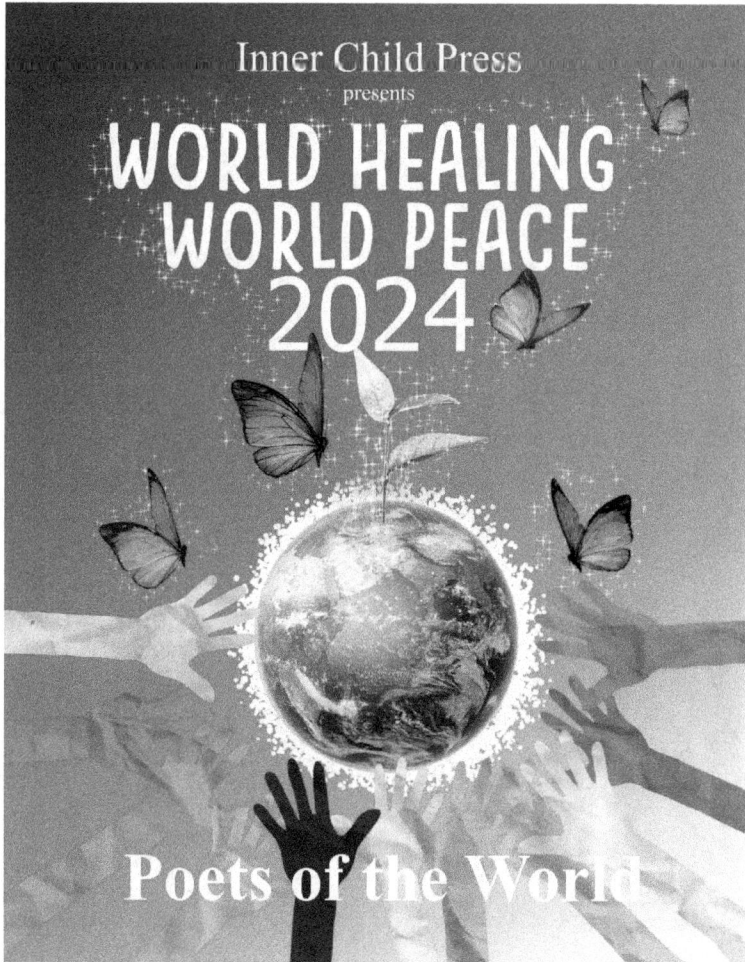

Inner Child Press
presents

WORLD HEALING
WORLD PEACE
2024

Poets of the World

www.innerchildpress.com/world-healing-world-peace-poetry

Preface

We, **Inner Child Press International, The Year of the Poet** and **The Poetry Posse** welcome you

WOW . . . a decade +. We continue to be excited as we have now crossed over into our 11th year of Production for **The Year of the Poet**.

This particular year we have chosen to feature renowned poets of history. We do hope you enjoy. Read ~ Learn.

For those of you who are not familiar with our story, back in 2013, a few of us poets got together with the simple intention of producing a book a month. That was our challenge. Since that time the enterprise has blossomed and brought forth a fruit that seems to keep on growing as evidenced as we enter 2023.

Our purpose is simple. Through our lyrical words and verse, we not only wish to share our poetic works, but we also have the poetic naiveté to believe that we can assist in the growth of consciousness of the things that have an effect our collective humanity. Therefore, we welcome your readership. For more about what we are attempting to accomplish, have a look at our Publishing Web Site . . . www.innerchildpress.com. If you would like to know a bit more about this particular endeavor please stop by for a visit at :

www.innerchildpress.com/the-year-of-the-poet

Over the years, Inner Child Press has been socially active to bring awareness and catalog through literature the things that have an impact upon our world and its inhabitants. We have solicited, produced, underwritten and published quite a few volumes to that end. For more insight you may wish to visit : www.innerchildpress.com/the-anthology-market. If you are a writer, poet, or activist, you would be advised to keep a eye out for upcoming volumes should you desire to participate. All readers are welcomed as well. Note, that there is a myriad of published volumes that are available as a FREE PDF download as well as available for purchase at affordable prices.

We at this time extend to you our well wishes for your own personal journey and hope that you consider including us as a travel companion.

Bless Up

Bill

William S. Peters, Sr.

Publisher
Inner Child Press International
www.innerchildpress.com

Renowned Poets
Pablo Neruda
1904 ~ 1973
July 2024

by hülya n. yılmaz, Ph.D.

Neftalí Ricardo Reyes Basoalto was already writing poetry at the age of 10. His mother had passed away shortly after his birth, and his surviving parent, his father, strongly discouraged him from writing, showing no interest in his poems. Hence, the pseudonym "Pablo Neruda" emerged, which the poet legally adopted in 1946.

The Chilean poet was renowned for his love poems, which he conveyed through metaphors and imagery inspired by nature. Literary critics and scholars in the field claim his most famous collection of love poems to be *Twenty Love Poems and a Song of Despair*. The key to his poetic uniqueness lies in his passion for life experiences and his distinctive way of expressing them in verse. His poetry distinguished itself due to his abandoning standard syntax, rhyme, and stanzaic organization.

Neruda was influenced by Surrealism in developing his enigmatic literary style. His poetic works showcase personal and collective anguish, nightmarish visions of disintegration, chaos, decay, and death; thus, they depict a contemporary descent into hell.

Neruda, who was also a diplomat and politician, was awarded the Nobel Prize for Literature two years before his death.

Finale*

Matilde, years or days
sleeping, feverish,
here or there,
gazing off,
twisting my spine,
bleeding true blood,
perhaps I awaken
or am lost, sleeping:
hospital beds, foreign windows,
white uniforms of the silent walkers,
the clumsiness of feet.

And then, these journeys
and my sea of renewal:
your head on the pillow,
your hands floating
in the light, in my light,
over my earth.

It was beautiful to live
when you lived!

The world is bluer and of the earth
at night, when I sleep
enormous, within your small hands.

* The last poem by Pablo Neruda, written shortly before his death, was found on his desk after his death and published posthumously. The poem is a love letter to his wife, Matilde; translated by William O'Daly from *The Sea and the Bells*.

hülya n. yılmaz, Ph.D.

Professor Emerita, Liberal Arts (PSU, U.S.A.)

Director of Editing Services, Inner Child Press International (U.S.A.)

Selected Sources:

Encyclopedia Britannica
NobelPrize.org
Biography.com
Wikipedia

Poets . . .
sowing seeds in the
Conscious Garden of Life,
that those who have yet to come
may enjoy the Flowers.

Poets, Writers . . . know that we are the enchanting magicians that nourishes the seeds of dreams and thoughts . . . it is our words that entice the hearts and minds of others to believe there is something grand about the possibilities that life has to offer and our words tease it forth into action . . . for you are the Poet, the Writer to whom the Gift of Words has been entrusted . . .

~ wsp

poetry is . . .

Poetry succeeds where instruction fails.

~ wsp

Now Available

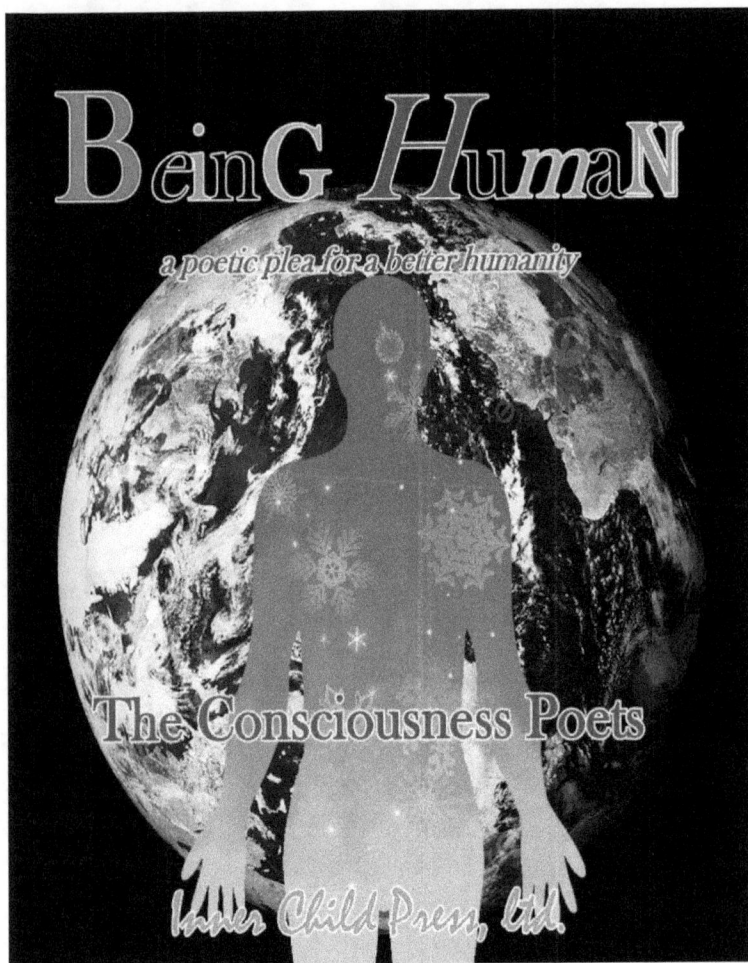

BeinG HumaN

a poetic plea for a better humanity

The Consciousness Poets

Inner Child Press, Ltd.

www.innerchildpress.com/the-anthology-market.com

Gail Weston Shazor

Gail Weston Shazor is a lover of words. She is fond of the arcane, unusual and the not yet words.

Coining words at an early age, there was often a bit of trouble with teachers, but she always had her mother and aunt to back up her choices in expression. Born in Mississippi, she spent her early years with her grandparents. Each of the four left very careful influences on her pre-schooling. She learned in turn how women worked in and out of the home and how men worked in and out of the home to support the family. She learned that a lack of proper schooling was not the only way to learn and understanding life was a great teacher. As in most rural families of color, women had a greater chance of formal learning. Both of Gail's grandmothers read out loud to the family whether it was the bible or the newspapers and important documents to their spouses.

Gail Weston Shazor has authored (so far) Notes from the Blue Roof, A Overstanding of an Imperfect Love, HeartSongs and Lies My Grandfather's Told Me. The number of anthologies is too many to list with the premier accomplishment of one of the contributors to The Year of The Poet. Gail will always lend her ink to community projects and will purchase the books of fellow poets in the Inner Child Press family.

There is no song of despair
Grief is in the imagination

I move far away to the unseen
And you cannot fathom my location

It is in this that you must find your way
For I am no longer your true north

I have furled my sails
So there is no covering for your soul

Fly, my love, into your destiny
Until I am but a memory

Open Mic ....Pantoum

It all started with a silver microphone
A dare from a friend in the group
She sent me up there all alone
To let my words do what they do

A dare from a friend in the group
I stood behind the stand
To let my words do what they do
And that's where this affair began

I stood behind the stand
Gripping the mic and easing up to the tip
And that's where this affair began
With a slow lick of my lips

Gripping the mic and easing up to the tip
Letters from my mind began to flow
With a slow lick of my lips
Maybe it was the shape, who knows

Letters from my mind began to flow
A treasure from my personal trove
Maybe it was the shape, who knows
But from that moment I was in love

She sent me up there all alone
Now my hand is ever ready to reach
It all started with a silver microphone
Thank you and "that's that piece"

Letters to my Muse

The closeness of your skin comforts me
You honor my quiet with one of your own
Keeping my words attached to
The paper as my paper
Must be contained in notebooks
You free my mind
To wander across worlds and return
With arms of letters
 I use some and then
Save the others for you
For creativity breeds and nothing is useless
Letters
Comfort
I find this in your space
And the graciousness of your breath
I imagine how this will sound
When I speak them to you at their birth
When they are ready to be heard
Until then you nurture them with kisses
Unexpected kisses
Welcomed kisses
One day the letters in my heart
Will come forth
And you will know that I too Love you.

Alicja Maria Kuberska

Alicja Maria Kuberska

Alicja Maria Kuberska – awarded Polish poetess, novelist, journalist, editor.

She is a member of the Polish Writers Associations in Warsaw, Poland and IWA Bogdani, Albania. She is also a member of directors' board of Soflay Literature Foundation, Our Poetry Archive (India) and Cultural Ambassador for Poland (Inner Child Press, USA)

Her poems have been published in numerous anthologies and magazines in : Poland, Czech Republic, Slovakia, Hungary,Ukraina, Belgium, Bulgaria, Albania, Spain, the UK, Italy, the USA, Canada, the UK, Argentina, Chile, Peru, Israel, Turkey, India, Uzbekistan, South Korea, Taiwan, China, Australia, South Africa, Zambia, Nigeria

She received two medals - the Nosside UNESCO Competition in Italy (2015) and European Academy of Science Arts and Letters in France (2017). Ahe also received a reward of international literary competition in Italy „ Tra le parole e 'elfinito" (2018). She was announced a poet of the 2017 year by Soflay Literature Foundation (2018).She also received : Bolesław Prus Prize Poland (2019), Culture Animator Poland (2019) and first prize Premio Internazionale di Poesia Poseidonia- Paestrum Italy (2019).

Pablo Neruda . . . Strange death

Between successive blue skies
death takes on many masks
It looks into eyes
and injects poison into veins.
In official communications
- cancer and malnutrition,
although the body denies the lies

The truth hidden in the corpse,
pierces the shell of lies,
hatches with pain
and points
a bony finger at the murderer.

Through the corridors of a military hospital
wandering shadows
whisper conspiratorially:
Augusto Pinochet, Michael Townley

Craiova

On a hot day
time stopped on the park avenue
It shook off the seconds
like jasmine petals
and arranged white collages
on the grass

In the shade of blooming lindens
the chess pieces
were getting ready for battle.
Did they devise a battle strategy
    –   the Queen's Gambit?

At the poet's monument
poems and bees sang.
Someone put a red peony
on Mihail Eminescu's chest
...the poet's heart throbbed

Sleepless Night

The minutes tremble on this starry night
The clock slowly advances the seconds,
stopping every now and then
- as if it didn't want to leave
the past day behind.

The wind outside the window
intertwines with the tree branches.
It shakes off the leaves
and sings a serenade louder and louder,
as if I it wanted
to charm the cold and distant Luna.

An inconspicuous nightingale
trills to the sky
It pierces the darkness
and wind with a vibrating voice
It will not rest until it touches
the stars with its song

Jackie
Davis
Allen

Jackie Davis Allen

Jackie Davis Allen, otherwise known as Jacqueline D. Allen or Jackie Allen, grew up in the Cumberland Mountains of Appalachia. As the next eldest daughter of a coal miner father and a stay at home mother, she was the first in her family to attend and graduate from college. Her siblings, in their own right, are accomplished, though she is the only one, to date, that has discovered the gift of writing.

Graduating from Radford University, with a Bachelor's of Science degree in Early Education, she taught in both public and private schools. For over a decade she taught private art classes to children both in her home and at a local Art and Framing Shop where she also sold her original soft sculptured Victorian dolls and original christening gowns.

She resides in northern Virginia with her husband, taking much needed get-aways to their mountain home near the Blue Ridge Mountains, a place that evokes memories of days spent growing up in the Appalachian Mountains.

A lover of hats, she has worn many. Following marriage to her college sweetheart, and as wife, mother, grandmother, teacher, tutor, artist, writer, poet and crafter, she is a lover of art and antiques, surrounding herself, always, with books, seeking to learn more.

In 2015 she authored *Looking for Rainbows, Poetry, Prose and Art*, and in 2017, *Dark Side of the Moon*. Both books of mostly narrative poetry were published by Inner Child Press and were edited by hulya n. yilmaz in 2019, *No Illusions. Through the Looking Glass*, which was nominated to be considered for a Pulitzer Prize by the publisher and editor of Inner Child Press, ltd.

http://www.innerchildpress.com/jackie-davis-allen.php
jackiedavisallen.com

A Means to Satisfy His Thirst

Rare is the man, or woman
Who wins poetry's greatest prize.
And yet, history proclaims
Pablo Neruda was such a man.

An activist, an agnostic, a communist,
Devoid of faith, trust
In any other but himself.
This the poet claims.

His poetry, today, still remains,
As a gift, a God given talent, far beyond others,
acknowledged, or not.
This is the man, from whose pen,

Poetry, seemingly, effortlessly, flowed forth.

The Angular Distance

The fog lies low over the mountains,
and now enshrouds me.

Invisible branches embrace
the gray morning ethereal,
and misty tears break through

though I attempt to hold them back.

My world is shattered,
my vision obscured.

How shall I find my way?
Ah, the Sun rises, my day reconstructed
but vaporous musings still dwell within.

Sobbing and heaving, I greet the dawn,

Even as joyful memories evoke
a smile, a dichotomy.

I strive to revisit the fog,
a world of my mind's own making;
yet the light, sublime

reveals a different path!

Hear Me, O Lord

I've come, bruised and empty,
searching for that
which once quenched
my thirst,
longing to be relieved
of the emptiness that consumes my every thought.

I am crying, mourning the loss of my creative voice.

Yielded up and waiting,
I silently mouth the words,
praying that once again
the poetic waters may flow,
even as I await your perfect Will.
I am determined to stay on bended knee

If that is what it takes.

Why is it that the flowers
continue to bloom,
and the rains still fall,
yet within me that which once flourished
seems wilted, dead or dying?
Do you hear me crying?
Father, I am here!

Do with me as you please.

Tzemin Ition Tsai

Dr. Tzemin Ition Tsai comes from the Republic of China(Taiwan). In addition to being a professor of literature at a university, he is more committed to writing poems, novels, and proses. He is also an editor of "Reading, Writing and Teaching" academic text, an International editor of "Contemporary dialogues" literary periodical in Macedonia, and Vice-Chairman of the International Jury of the SAHITTO INTERNATIONAL AWARD in Bangladesh, and a columnist for "Chinese Language Monthly" in Taiwan.

In a wide range of literary creations, he is particularly fond of interesting stories or novels, and writing articles or poems about the feelings of nature and human beings. He has won many national literary awards. His literary works have been anthologized and published in books, journals, and newspapers in more than 55 countries and have been translated into more than 24 languages.

Delicate Heart and Intentions

Spring, with the vermilion countenance of a chicory bloom,
None may identify it.
Lingering sorrow, a vast expanse of mountains and rivers,
Unasked, only the tugged fragrance, slightly tart.
Upon the rock, the flowers sip the faint dew, this heart yet
refuses to smile.
Heaven's love, carried by the wind,
Creates inexplicable tears, a few lines streaking the cheeks.
In the northwest,
Rain drifts, the wooden door barely ajar beside the lonely
inn.
Silken spring flowers seem to lose their way, falling into
the garden's crevice.
Pretending indifference, not stained by a touch of affection,
still a bee gathers alone.
The red petals fall on the water, the sound of the wind
gradually softens.
Red flowers sway in fruiting, not willing to let the lonely
dream of the leaves on the branch look outward.
The mountains, the deep, distant, and shallow shadows of
mist.
A corner of the ancient house, concealing the lazy flowers.
Beneath the great tree, no lamps are seen, gazing at the
silent millennia.
The main gate tightly locks dreams, for decades,
Not traversed by anyone.
The water's surface is tranquil in the distance, an ethereal
life.
How faint,
Half asleep or awake, the wind blows past. Who should
respond to this sound?

Silken spring flowers cover my delicate charm, how bearable?
For with the wind's desire to fly, parched earth buries the sandy mound.
And the clouds, should they not know?
The heart, upon its arrival, if bound, only grows more desolate.
The reluctant heart, meaningless purity, idle chatter paints the lips with rouge and powder.

Embark On the Delicate Of Poetry

The noise floats up alone, the corner of the city.
Listening to the whispers of the wind. The poets are silent.
Nestled in the sunlight-kissed grains of May's dawn,
A subtle warmth emerges — obscure or
illuminated emotions, lost in the fragments beneath the
quill.

Atop the mirror lake, under the resting clouds,
Drunken by rubbing, the poet writes lovingly.
Thoughts — now concealed, now unveiled — ebb and flow
like rainbows,
Echoing the tranquil silhouettes in gentle whispers.
The rhythm endures, despite wandering strokes.

Unearthing emotional veins from rugged words,
Roaming the sea of letters, cherished crystal phrases
shimmer.
From sacrifice, a unique rhythm is birthed,
A poet or a relentless craftsman?
Heart swaying, drunk on the inky scent of morning dew.

The Song of the Cloud Gate

I look up at the cloud gate,
And I see the world in a new way.
The clouds are like waves,
And the sky is like an ocean.
I feel small and insignificant,
But I am also
Part of something much bigger than myself.

I am part of the universe,
And I am connected
To everything around me.
I am filled with a sense of peace and awe,
And I know that I am loved.

I am grateful for the opportunity
To see the world in a new way.
I am grateful for the gift of life,
And I am grateful
For the love that surrounds me.

I will never forget the feeling
Of looking up at the cloud gate,
And I will never forget the song that it sang to me.

Tzemin Ition Tsai

Shareef Abdur Rasheed

Shareef Abdur Rasheed

Shareef Abdur-Rasheed, AKA Zakir Flo was born and raised in Brooklyn, New York. His education includes Brooklyn College, Suffolk County Community College and Makkah, Saudi Arabia. He is a Veteran of the Viet Nam era, where in 1969 he reverted to his now reverently embraced Islamic Faith. He is very active in the Islamic community and beyond with his teachings, activism and his humanity.

Shareef's spiritual expression comes through the persona of "Zakir Flo" . Zakir is Arabic for "To remind". Never silent, Shareef Abdur-Rasheed is always dropping science, love, consciousness and signs of the time in rhyme.

Shareef is the Patriarch of the Abdur-Rasheed Family with 9 Children (6 Sons and 3 Daughters) and 41 Grandchildren (24 Boys and 17 Girls).

For more information about Shareef, visit his personal FaceBook Page at :

https://www.facebook.com/shareef.abdurrasheed1
https://zakirflo.wordpress.com

Pablo Neruda the fearless
B. July 12, 1904
D. Sept. 23, 1973

words that resonate
words that inspire
more than one can artist of
painting words conceive
believe it, it's true
"the pen is mightier
then the sword"
his countries world
renown master poet
also, freedom fighter,
human rights, civil and
human rights activist,
warrior
yes, indeed pride of
Chile
Nobel prize in
literature 1971
international peace
prize 1950 etc.
but that's a small
slice
diplomat, politician
member Chilean
Communist party,
yes, a known gifted
poet from 13 years
young
talking styles certainly
variety
including, romantic,
political, historical, etc.

his love oriented could
passionate yet metaphoric
if a women's love abandoned
him and left his life he had
other loves for instance
rage against the machine
that being oppressive
governments, rulers
who deny rights God
given
therefore, he will not
be despondent
he gave his life for
others to be free
" The pen is mightier
then the sword"

Unleashed..

forces released
wreak havoc
on earth as we speak
or quicker then we think
Shaitan his forces set upon
mankind
bet on man is blind
open ya eyes mankind
open ya eyes
spiritually blind mankind
worse kinda blind
starve the flesh feed the soul
recipe to stay whole
regain control
retain the role
starve the flesh feed the soul
past the test pass go
let the world go
get the gusto
what it is if you know
starve the flesh feed the soul
goes like this
eternal bliss
gotz ta get some of this

entitlement..,

means, meant time wasted spent
thinking you the best thing after
the white bread invents
world wars event
you supposed ta get mosta
there is to get
on the strength of your color,
family, tribe, nation, possessions,
all arrogant inventions
manifest from evil intentions
that you and yours are the best
separate, apart from the rest
a lie first perpetuated by the
main pest
the personification of evil
the devil himself promotes his
traits on the human race
just scan the human landscape
proliferation of evil traits
lies, deception, greed, manipulation,
violence, genocide, no justification
pure indifference, hate
man against man
nation against nation
promoting justification of entitlement
for certain persuasions, affiliations
on the basis of pure arrogance,
ignorance
ever since, from time memorial
never any evidence to support
imperialism, racism, nationalism,
tribalism, and all the other schisms

that saturate all of man's ism's
such is this world always was
always will
fact remains it's insane
always the same deal
Until the creator puts a stop to
this game of evil

Noreen Snyder

Noreen Snyder

Noreen Ann Snyder has been writing since she was a teenager. She writes a variety of different topics. Her favorite poetic forms are Sonnets, Blitz, Haiku, Tanka, and Free Verse. She always learning different poetic forms.

Noreen Ann Snyder is a poet, writer, and an author of five books, (four books are co-authored with her late husband, Garry A. Snyder.) Her poetry is in several Inner Child Press Anthologies. She is the founder ofThe Poetry Club on Facebook.

Pablo Neruda

Pablo Neruda was a Chilean Poet
Diplomat and Politician,
one of the great 20th Century Poets
who won the 1971 Nobel Prize in Literature.
He wrote various genres including
love poetry, political manifestos,
surrealist poetry, historical epics,
a prose autobiography and odes.
What he is saying to us
through his poetry
is that we all can speak out
and not be afraid
of what we believe in
through our poetry
and that is a necessity.

Close to Orchestra

hold me tight
hold me close
close and firm
close to your heart
heart of gold
heart beating fast
fast and slow
fast lovers
lovers lane
lovers forever
forever we'll be true
forever I'll love you
you are my world
you are precious
precious as a gem
precious as poems
poems from the heart
poems of love
love me tender
love so true
true to my word
true as vows
vows of marriage
vows unbroken
unbroken heart
unbroken promises
promises of success
promises of marriage
marriage and love
marriage is give and take
take me as I am
take me now

now is the time
now not tomorrow
tomorrow I'll be here
tomorrow might come
come with me
come here
here it is
here is my key
key to my heart
key to my soul
soul and spirit
soul mate for life
life is grand
life like an orchestra
orchestra music is beautiful
orchestra music like love
love
beautiful

Life

Loving you is easy to do

Learning to live without you

like almost nearly impossible

Life will go on, it is hard.

Lament I'll try not to do instead

listen to God; He'll help me through.

Lessons to remember we all will die.

Listen, be prepared and that's life.

Noreen Snyder

Elizabeth E. Castillo

Elizabeth Esguerra Castillo

Elizabeth Esguerra Castillo is a multi-awarded and an Internationally-Published Contemporary Author/Poet and a Professional Writer / Creative Writer / Feature Writer / Journalist / Travel Writer from the Philippines. She has 2 published books, "Seasons of Emotions" (UK) and "Inner Reflections of the Muse", (USA). Elizabeth is also a co-author to more than 60 international anthologies in the USA, Canada, UK, Romania, India. She is a Contributing Editor of Inner Child Magazine, USA and an Advisory Board Member of Reflection Magazine, an international literary magazine. She is a member of the American Authors Association (AAA) and PEN International.

Web links:

Facebook Fan Page

https://free.facebook.com/ElizabethEsguerraCastillo

Google Plus

https://plus.google.com/u/0/+ElizabethCastillo

Do No Forget Me, Neruda

Neruda, his verses struck the heart

Through pain, sorrow, glee, and feelings of love

He never fails to evoke strong emotions of his readers

Neruda once said "love without understanding is not love at
all..."

For how can one love another without knowing him first?

Though despair at times is his constant companion,

Pablo knows how to make fun of himself through his
evocative verses

Making him the Creative Legend that we call came to
know.

Undefined Love

Dawn is about to set
Here I am still thinking of you
Your shadow vanishing in the moonlit night,
I walked the dark path to realize you're not there
Were you just an illusion, a dream, or were created by just
pure imagination
All I know is that you possess those pair of eyes that
glimmer in the dark
That even if I get lost anywhere in this world, I may find
myself again in you,
You're more than the word Love itself for I cannot simply
define how you swept me off my feet
A meager stare from you sets my heart in so much
commotion
And hearing you call my name in such an intricate way sets
my soul on fire,
Find me again, take my hand and let's go to the end of the
world
There at the tower let us watch the moon while some
clouds dance in the background
As the splashing of waves make sounds while we walk by
the shoreline barefooted,
Feeling the warm sand beneath our feet with a mild breeze
brushing our cheeks
Find me again in another lifetime where we could define
this eternal love we share transcending time and space.

Lovers Under the Moonlight

Let us walk to the ends of the Earth,
You and I, hand in hand
Forget all our cares and be One
Be One with the Universe,
With the Moon as our witness
Its luminescence guides our path
To a place where Love resides forever.
Lovers under the moonlight,
We are lost stars dancing in the eddies
Connected souls by the cosmic dots,
Your serene face is illuminated by its hypnotizing auras
A halo highlighting your angelic countenance
I see you in my midsummer dream,
Our love was born to a mystical alchemy.
With the beauteous moon in sight,
We dance like there is no tomorrow
You and I on a mystic flight
A much-awaited alchemical marriage.

Mutawaf Shaheed

Mutawaf Shaheed

C. E. Shy has been writing since the seventh grade. He continued writing through high school, until he became more involved in sports. After his graduation, he worked at the White Motors Company where he wrote for the company's newspaper. He started a column called: "The Poet's Corner." That was his first published work.

www.innerchildpress.com/c-e-shy.php

Pablo Neruda

Good advice is a spice of life.
Enjoy it before it changes.

Wisdom follows knowledge
to a trail that leads to sound
conclusions.

Not too far away in the Amazon
are recipes for healing.

A place full of poetry
living among the trees that
make it not so foreboding.

Inspired by unfamiliar smells
and sounds that let one know
you're not alone.

Like a laboratory where the mind
can bend without breaking.

Where thoughts are provoked.
He stored them in life's library.

Loan Sharks

The loss of income has an outcome, and then
here comes the repo man to take back your van.
The dirty louse that took your house has an office
at the bank.
He's sitting there to yank your chain to make it plain
that you can have the house at higher interest rates.
He can't disguise the lying eyes that sit behind the
desk.
Don't miss the penalty clause that states the laws of
diminishing returns.
The wife must have that picket fence and you must
get another job to pay for the evidence.

Passed- SAMF

Pitching mental pennies at past passions.
They bounce off rubber walls, to be struck
by liquid lightning for raising their heads again.
I remember the passion that was underpinned by pity.
Sometimes they called it loose love.
Square business had a way of correcting itself
taking the edges off when it could.
Surrounding twisted theories so they could fit
inside the heads of maniacs whose stupidity
protrudes from their undigested breath.
Minds bleed from being handpicked. Antics being
performed by semantics while eating
medical breakfasts in the backseats of limos driven
by serial killers dressed in the color of money.
Smelling jokes that are not funny enough to make
one laugh. The tears dried before they could reach
the eyes of kind men and ladies.
Flower gardens grow now from profane fertilizer as
stereo-types crisscross. Across the full spectrum,
standup comics dominate the podiums as the crowds
wait in line to celebrate being blindsided.
Rivers dry up and the land disappears the sea waters
rise and the dumb bells cheer. Saying, "the rocket ships
will get us out of here!" I don't think so SAMF.

hülya
n.
yılmaz

Of Turkish descent, hülya n. yılmaz [sic] is Professor Emerita (Penn State, U.S.A.), Director of Editing Services (Inner Child Press International, U.S.A.), and a trilingual literary translator. Before her poetry and prose publications, she authored an extensive research book in German on cross-cultural literary influences.

Her works of literature include a trilingual collection of poems, memoirs in verse, prose poetry, short stories, a bilingual poetry book, and two books of poetry (one, co-authored). Her poetic offerings appeared in numerous anthologies of global endeavors.

hülya writes creatively to attain and nourish a comprehensive awareness for and development of our humanity.

hülya n. yılmaz, a traveler on the journey called "life" . . .

Writing Web Site
https://hulyanyilmaz.com/

Editing Web Site
https://hulyasfreelancing.com

Sur. . .

realism,
revolutionising
human experience;
a rational vision of life, on one hand;
on the other hand, the unconscious and dreams . . .

Breton, the father of surrealist art,
followed by Duchamp, Giacometti, Klee, Ernst,
and many more. Not forgetting Neruda . . .

Anguish over disintegration,
chaos, decay, and death

To personally experience these nightmares,
but also collectively . . .

Sur . . .
realism

the dead and the living*

my mother's grave, lost

too many look-alikes since then

yet his dog finds his

*Inspired in 2012 by the news of a dog refusing to leave his owner's grave for six years.

dying to life

heart slows its beat
blood rushes to head
at every grasp of the loss
asleep, awake,
or in a dream state

ears deafen to sounds
eyes, blind to colors
voice trembles by steady tears
food serves to deaden the thirst

elation departs

eternal craving remains behind
and keeps on and on and . . .

death comes
oh, yes! It comes
but to kill

it condemns to life
the undying void inside

Teresa E. Gallion

Teresa E. Gallion

Teresa E. Gallion was born in Shreveport, Louisiana and moved to Illinois at the age of 15. She completed her undergraduate training at the University of Illinois Chicago and received her master's degree in Psychology from Bowling Green State University in Ohio. She retired from New Mexico state government in 2012.

She moved to New Mexico in 1987. While writing sporadically for many years, in 1998 she started reading her work in the local Albuquerque poetry community. She has been a featured reader at local coffee houses, bookstores, art galleries, museums, libraries, Outpost Performance Space, the Route 66 Festival in 2001 and the State of Oklahoma's Poetry Festival in Cheyenne, Oklahoma in 2004. She occasionally hosts an open mic.

Teresa's work is published in numerous Journals and anthologies. She has two CDs: *On the Wings of the Wind* and *Poems from Chasing Light*. She has published three books: *Walking Sacred Ground, Contemplation in the High Desert* and *Chasing Light*.

Chasing Light was a finalist in the 2013 New Mexico/Arizona Book Awards.

The surreal high desert landscape and her personal spiritual journey influence the writing of this Albuquerque poet. When she is not writing, she is committed to hiking the enchanted landscapes of New Mexico. You may preview her work at

http://bit.ly/1aIVPNq or *http://bit.ly/13IMLGh*

Homage to Pablo Neruda

When I think of love poems,
I think of the delicate balance
of your words flowing through me.

Between shadow and light,
my soul plays with you on the page.
Pablo your lyrics dance around my bed
to the tune of ecstasy.

Flowers hide behind the trees
to peek at your words.
They feel the power of loves embrace
close to the heart of each blossom.

Red wine runs down your lips
like the blood of first love.
Tears swell in clusters
as you and I unite as one
and morning light burns your chest.

You call forth my imagination
as I stare into January light
crackling in the fireplace.
A fresh season is brewing
under the snow blanket outside
and I want to hibernate here with you Pablo
until the spring daffodils toot their horns.

Falling into Grace

He locks his gaze on her naked lips
and her smile burst into flames.
The heat of the exposure burns
down to her breast.

Her legs freeze in place.
She cannot detach from his gaze.
The heart pumps purple violets.
Rainbow colors dance on the ground.

He speaks to her without words.
Breathe in and accept binding grace.
She complies and falls without fear
into the arms of the Beloved.

Attached by Love

The clock is ticking toward heaven.
I need you here in the present moment.
Surrender your fears and frustrations.
Take off your paranoid boots.

Come play in the garden
of mischief, humor and laughter.
We can make memories
to carry back home to God.

I see you running in the desert sand.
Your hair sings in the breeze.
So I close my eyes
and feel your feet touch the sand.

Ashok K. Bhargava

ASHOK BHARGAVA is a poet, writer, inspirational speaker and a literary consultant. He has attended poetry conferences in Italy, Turkey, India and Philippines. His latest book "Riding the Tide" about his battle with cancer has been translated and published in Arabic, Hindi, Telugu and Bengali languages. He is a contributing writer to several anthologies worldwide including World Poetry Almanac 2014. He has been published in numerous print and online magazines.

Ashok has won many accolades including Poet Ambassador to Japan, Kalidasa International award, World Poetry Lifetime Achievement award, Writers Beyond Borders Peace award and Tapsilog Leadership award for his community involvement. He is founder of Writers International Network Canada Society to discover, nourish, recognize and celebrate writers, poets and artists and to assist them to network with the community at large. He is the author of eight books of poetry and one anthology. He is Artist-in-Residence at Moberly Arts & Cultural Centre and also co-edits the literary section of The Link Newspaper.

Praise for Pablo
For Pablo Neruda

You're not peripheral
You belong here.
You can't be just pushed away.

Like winged seeds
You'll continue to glide to everywhere
Put down your roots and flourish.

You may turn your back
Like the sails
To opposing winds to push forward.

I see you not as a prisoner
But a liberator and crusader
For your people.

If I

If I could see
through your eyes
it would be a world
of different laughs and cries.

If I could feel
through your heart
I would feel different joys
that might make my sadness depart.

If I could understand
the world through your mind
I might experience contentment
and leave my sorrows behind.

But if you could love me
the way I do
I guarantee
it would change the world
for you and me.

I wish things were different
than they are.

If only I could …

Totally Timeless

Are we breaking-up
No
Are we leaving behind
Our old 'Selves'
No

Are we walking
In the same place
Returning to our steps
In search of lost time and space

Or in a circle
Where beginning and end are confused
Past and present
Cutting out the unattainable future

Where can I find you
Just not to be lost to me
As if you died
And I
Mourning and mourning
For those who are alive

Let me hear your voice
Now
How I feel
In my dreams

Where a swallow
always brings with her
a little spring sky
even if it's autumn

In the happy confusion
Past and present
Space and time

Ashok K. Bhargava

Caroline 'Ceri Naz' Nazareno Gabis

Caroline 'Ceri' Nazareno-Gabis

Caroline 'Ceri Naz' Nazareno-Gabis, author of Velvet Passions of Calibrated Quarks, World Poetry Canada International Director to Philippines is a multi-awarded poet, editor, journalist, educator, peace and women's advocate. She believes that learning other's language and culture is a doorway to wisdom.

Among her poetic belts include **Gabrielle Galloni Memorial Panorama International Youth Award 2022**, Panorama Youth Literary Awards 2020, 7th Prize Winner in the 19th, 20th and 21st Italian Award of Literary Festival; Writers International Network-Canada ''Amazing Poet 2015'', The Frang Bardhi Literary Prize 2014 (Albania), Poet Journalist Award 2014 (Tuzla, Istanbul, Turkey) and World Poetry Empowered Poet 2013 (Vancouver, Canada). She's a featured member of Association of Women's Rights and Development (AWID), The Poetry Posse, Galaktika Poetike, Asia Pacific Writers and Translators (APWT), Axlepino and Anacbanua. Her poetry and children's stories have been featured in different anthologies and magazines worldwide.

Links to her works:

http://panitikan.ph/2018/03/30/caroline-nazareno-gabis/

https://apwriters.org/author/ceri_naz/

http://www.aveviajera.org/nacionesunidasdelasletras/id1181.html

Neruda In My Mind

Neruda, your verses dance,
A tango of love desire, love lost,
Ink spills like raindrops on paper,
words are woven from the fabric of longing,
Your metaphors are secret artichokes of love,
some bloom like wildflowers,
each petal a passionate charm that resonates
the depths of your songs beyond cultures,
Your love, like ripe fruit,
drips from your lines,
 sweet and intoxicating.
The sea current echoes your name,
 you are the salt in our tears.
As we read your ideals that transcend time,
Neruda, your poems become nebula,
like the giant clouds, where stars are born or die,
But tonight, I trace your name with the constellations,
The interstellar syllables of my love for your words.

Mundivagant

I wander like a cosmic nomad,
drifting through stardust lanes,
My soul unshackled by gravity,
as twilight mirrors the constellation of wishes.
I trace through my fingertips,
mapping celestial highways,
Where galaxies collide in silent ballet,
and black holes sing their ancient songs.
My feet kiss moon-kissed soil,
 and I become a vagabond of existence,
 A wanderer between realms,
seeking secrets whispered by nebulae.
The universe unfurls its tapestry,
 each thread a story of birth and death,
 I, the mundivagant dreamer,
weave my verses into the void.
So I journey, untethered and wild,
 a comet trailing wonder,
 Chasing Infinity's elusive tail
 forever lost, forever found.

The Alchemist Whisper

Here's the land of dreams and reality,
The alchemist toils, his heart and hands,
With fire and with alembic mold,
He transmuted leaden sorrow into gold.
He whispers to the elements of light,
To reveal his spirit free,
In crucibles of hope,
A dance of shadows,
A journey to the ultimate quest.
He is a philosopher, extending his hands
To find the elixir of life,
Through pitfalls and storms,
His soul's alchemy, a field of wonders.
He is a seeker of truth,
Who turns mundane into a fountain of worth,
His heart dares to dream,
The alchemist's touch is like a stream.

Swapna Behera

Swapna Behera is a trilingual poet, translator, environmentalist, editor from India and author of seven books of different genres including one on children's literature on Environment. She is the recipient of International UGADI AWARD 2019, honoured from Gujurat Sahitya Akademi 2022, 2021 International Poesis Award of Honor as Jury, Pentasi B World Fellow Poet, Honoured Poet of India from Seychelles Government and International awards from Algeria, Morocco, Kajhakhstan, modern Arabic Literary Renaissance of Egypt, International Arts Council Argentina etc. Her stories, poems, articles are published in many International and National magazines and ezines. Her poem A NIGHT IN THE REFUGEE CAMP is translated into 67 languages. She has received over 60 National and International Awards. At present she is the Cultural Ambassador for India and South Asia of Inner Child and the life member of Odisha Environmental Society

Email
swapna.behera@gmail.com

Web Site
http://swapnabehera.in/

Pablo Neruda: a legacy maker

the Latin American poet
his sonnets speak volumes of love
"here I love you"
romanticism at its climax
"I want to be with you what spring does with cherry trees"
a Chilean poet best known for his poems
expressed through metaphors and images of nature
a political activist
who helped thousands of Republican refugees
escape to Chile after Spanish civil War
"I love you without knowing you"
his writings brought great social change
he was awarded the noble prize
a public figure, an activist and a senator
his verdict was
surround yourself with inspiration
discomfort breeds new perspective
a combination of purpose and hard work
that is why he is a legacy maker
to codify love, time, destruction and loneliness
filled with both harmony and anguish ideas of social decay
isolation, alienation, communism and oppression
laughter is the language of soul
dying slowly is when you don't travel or read
listen to the sounds of life
life itself is a legacy
isn't it ?

in the Manikarnika ghat

the masculine bones
never give the full stop
the feminine breasts
never ends the perimeter of death
the pediatric bones hip hop on the cement pandal
death tunes at tandem with life
the aghoris smoke taking fire from the pyre
drinks from the bowls of dried human skull
the bohemian attitude of who cares
the tinkling bell and the mantras of last ritual
with visible marigold flower stitched with banana stem
strings
robust, sick, cancer patients
old or young
bodies lie down on the bamboo stretcher made up of six
pieces
carried by muscle men
decorated with vermillion, red clothes
pure ghee the authentic smell of the ghat with the camphor
and the smell of the burning flesh
does this ghat serve Nirvana ashes half born flesh and body
the carcass putrefying flesh
the corpse beyond the boundaries
spread the anthem of tears
the relatives shave the head
the pundits do the rituals
death is celebrated here as liberation and salvation
everyday around three hundred bodies are burnt
this ghat is a sacred cremation site
mourners take the bath
the Ganga digests the pain ,anguish ,the flesh and ash
the mysterious ghat

that breaks the cycle of birth and rebirth
the abandoned coins, stale flower garlands and bones
only witness of life cycle
death and life parallel to each other
if there is life
then certainly life speaks
the history and geography of a river
that can gulp tons of pollution
mystery of a river that blesses the civilization

e.g manikarnika ghat is the cremation ground located on the river banks of river Ganga

aghoris:- aghoris are monists who seek liberation from the cycle of life and death

save me from the dead zone

hello, hello
 am speaking from the dead zone
dear all
here is my appeal
I wish to live
I am in the ocean where the dissolved oxygen is depleted
I cannot sustain
in this hypoxic condition
you are worried for your cellular dead zones
I am a tiny fish; give me little oxygen
I can recover
you throw pesticides that split nitrogen and phosphorous
can't you reverse the dead zones
stop oil spills in the ocean
change the farming practice
upgrade waste water treatment facilities
anthropogenic sources of radioactive create pollution
I love to live
I love to swim
I love activities
don't kill me
don't put me in the toxic zone
I appeal
save me from the dead zone

Swapna Behera

Albert 'Infinite' Carrasco

Albert "Infinite The Poet" Carrasco is an urban poet, mentor and public speaker.

Albert believes his experience of growing up in poverty, dealing with drugs and witnessing murder over and over were lessons learnt, in order to gain knowledge to teach. Albert's harsh reality and honesty is a powerfully packed punch delivered through rhyme. Infinite grew up in the east part of the Bronx and still resides there, so he knows many young men will follow the same dark path he followed looking for change. The life of crime should never be an option to being poor but it is, very often.

Infinite poetry @lulu.com

Alcarrasco2 on YouTube

Infinite the poet on reverbnation

Infinite Poetry

www.lulu.com/us/en/shop/al-infinite-carrasco/infinite-poetry/paperback/product-21040240.html

www.innerchildpress.com/albert-carrasco

Pablo Neruda

I was just a teen from Chile when I started to write poetry,
Writing was how I expressed my emotions freely.
My styles vary on how I feel at the moment, or what I'm
going through,
Politics might be on my mind, historical events,
or I just might want to say I love you.
During my years I was considered to be one of the most
influential of the time,
I was being listened to and read by people all over the
world because of the way
I painted pictures with my voices delivery and poetic lines.
Due to my passions of being a writer and a public figure
speaker,
In 1971 I was awarded the Nobel Prize in literature.
Mr. Pablo Neruda…. a Chilean Politician/word magician.

Life not a lifestyle

 opened up earlier and closed up later than the average hustler. I wasn't on temporary time. I wasn't out there scrambling for a pair of kicks and a new fit, I was thinkn longevity, like turn'n an 0 to 1000 after a few flips to get the fam out the hood while I stood in the bricks gettn this money. I wasn't tryn to build a block then stop because it's hot or because i already copped a whip, a Cuban and have a selection of thots. I was in the beginning stages of building an empire from the mixture of two powders, water and fire, I was out there morn to night whether it was sunny, snowing or raining with packs in the bushes and gats off safety on parked car tires. My nightmares of poverty led to actions to make dreams of being rich in or around NYCHA property become reality rather than just a closed eye fantasy. I was out there trap binge'n, breath hot, balls sweaty, ass smelly, I'm livn dirty to keep my pockets filthy and to break the generational curse so generations after me can be hereditarily wealthy. I'm getting locked up and going right back to the block, cribs are getting raided they're taking my money and work, it's was okay because I could copp caine with just my name to hit the spot to open up shop a few hours after locks were popped and doors dropped. Then it's back to binge'n so I can pay the plug for what my name just copped and my gems just chopped. There was set backs but I snapped back. I had two choices…. Hustle hard in these New York streets or impatiently wait for the first to eat.

Emulate the 8

Dudes try to emulate the 8 but peeps can't see my reflection in them. The bar is set to high, they can't pull up. I mean they try to live as if they're gettn that bag, as if they drip with swag, as if they're respected when they're basic... sons, I'm an international living legend if I must brag. I over stand, if I wasn't me, I would want to be like me, but we are not the same, time would have to be rewinded so you could grow up in poverty like me, lose a parent at twelve and deal with mourning pain, go through all the emotions, motions and rebellion that led me to the game. I want to stop shootn and look to the left or right and see your muzzle flame, I want to stand back in the kitchen and see you turn coke into hard caine, I want to see you boss up and have bells ringing when they speak your name... I know that'll never happen even if we could rewind time because dudes wouldn't be able to hold on to the reigns in the streets i reigned. I'm a ghost so when I do pop up and dudes see me they get star struck or frightened, I'm always on point but when I make appearances my senses are heightened, the grip on the pipe tightens, don't start none won't be none, dudes don't want smoke with me, if they do I'll hit em with the entire dispensary. I always come in peace but because of the life I lived my head will forever stay on a swivel like I got beef.

Michelle Joan Barulich

Michelle Joan Barulich

Michelle Joan Barulich was born in Honolulu, Hawaii on the island of Oahu. She started writing poetry and songs with her younger brother Paul. They have written many songs in their teen years. She is currently studying Alternative Medicine and would like to become a Homeopathic Doctor. Michelle loves all kinds of animals and birds; she does wild rehabilitation. She has also rescued rock pigeons that make great pets.

https://www.facebook.com/michelle.barulich

Pablo's Way

Pablo was a great writer
His poems were subtle and elegant
To better communicate
His new social concerns
To his readers
His development was interrupted by the Spanish civil war
One of his major works
Odas Elementals
The verses were simple
But direct and precise
Pablo won the Nobel Prize
For literature
He is perhaps
 The most important Latin American
Poet of the 20th century
Way to go Pablo Nervda!

Broken Memories

Somewhere, somehow
In the midst where shadows are plagued
Something has to break
Something has to ache
...And the rain we heard last night
Has now stopped, the sun shines through the drapes
Giving me a new emotion
Calling in about last night
Talking about how we danced
People whispered, "They really tripped the light fantastic"
Somewhere, somehow
In the midst where shadows play
Something has to give
Something has to take
Do you remember, how we played like children?
Laughing too, at our mistakes
Don't you recall how our minds used to work
How come we forget, is gaining knowledge the answer
why?
... But somewhere, somehow
In the midst where love is stored
Something has to live
Something has to die
Playing silly games and knowing the simple things
Rules didn't matter to us
Somewhere, somehow
In the midst where we all want to be
Something has to be trapped
Something has to be free
And our souls were at peace
Our minds reached new heights
Remembering about last night, how we danced
And all the people all around
 Whispered, "they're really tripping the light fantastic"..

Friends

I was alone, feeling sad
But shortly, I was among friends
Talking, laughing, and sharing our feelings
With one another
How it filled my soul
To be in a house with joy and excitement
Friends, are the best part of life
How I will remember that special day
The warmth in my heart still remains.

Eliza Segiet

Eliza Segiet graduated with a Master's Degree in Philosophy at Jagiellonian University.

Received *Global Literature Guardian Award* – from Motivational Strips, World Nations Writers Union and Union Hispanomundial De Escritores (UHE) 2018.

Nominated for the Pushcart Prize 2019, 2021.

Laureate *Naji Naaman Literary Prize 2020,*

International Award Paragon of Hope (2020),

World Award 2020 *Cesar Vallejo* for Literary Excellence. Laureate of the Special Jury *Sahitto International Award* 2021, World Award *Premiul Fănuş Neagu* 2021.

Finalist *Golden Aster Book* World Literary Prize 2020, *Mili Dueli* 2022, Voci nel deserto 2022.

At the international Festival of Poetry CAMPIONATO MONDIALE DI POESIA (2021/2022) she won the title of vice-champion of the world.

Award BHARAT RATNA RABINDRANATH TAGORE INTERNATIONAL AWARD (2022).

Award - *World Poets Association* (2023).

Laureate Between words and infinity *"International Literary Award (2023).*

Eliza Segiet

Realization
To the memory of Pablo Neruda*

Trees, rivers, cliffs,
snow-covered fields –
the Earth's gifts,
in combination
with solitude, emotion
and another man,
would inspire his soul,
directing his path towards a symbiosis
of Nature and Man,
and Man with himself.
He would say that a poet is not
a little god,
whilst others knew
that he was a Great Poet.
With his words he would awake
the world full of injustice,
realizing that
– darkness should change to *blossom.*

Pablo Neruda (12.07.1904 - 23 .09. 1973) Chilean poet, diplomat and politician who won the Nobel Prize for Literature in 1971. Neruda became known as a poet at the age of 13. He wrote in a variety of styles, including surrealist poems, historical epics, political manifestos, prose autobiography and passionate love poems

Translated by Dorota Stępińska

Illusion

I deluded myself that

it would still be summer.

And it stands

in a frame.

I stopped the time.

I am not looking for the sun.

I let myself be seduced by the illusion

that it does not set.

After all,

I can still roam

the trails of the past.

Translated by Artur Komoter

Imagination

When the memories
are still smouldering
and the memory allows
to return to the past,
what was
before
becomes a moment
to which it gladly returns.

It will not throw away
those days.
They cannot be forgotten.

One cannot dream through
loneliness,
but it can always
hug with hope.

Translated by Artur Komoter

William S. Peters Sr.

Bill's writing career spans a period of well over 50 years. Being first Published in 1972, Bill has since went on to Author in excess of 50+ additional Volumes of Poetry, Short Stories, etc., expressing his thoughts on matters of the Heart, Spirit, Consciousness and Humanity. His primary focus is that of Love, Peace and Understanding!

Bill says . . .

I have always likened Life to that of a Garden. So, for me, Life is simply about the Seeds we Sow and Nourish. All things we "Think and Do", will "Be" Cause and eventually manifest itself to being an "Effect" within our own personal "Existences" and "Experiences" . . . whether it be Fruit, Flowers, Weeds or Barren Landscapes! Bill highly regards the Fruits of his Labor and wishes that everyone would thus go on to plant "Lovely" Seeds on "Good Ground" in their own Gardens of Life!

to connect with Bill, he is all things Inner Child

www.iaminnerchild.com

Personal Web Site

www.iamjustbill.com

Pablo Neruda

With this pen
I declare my voice
Shall not embrace the silence,
Nor
Shall my love be restrained

Nay,
The machinations of life
Shall not hinder
The soul of who I am,
For I have retired
The persona of
Neftalí Ricardo Reyes Basoalto
And may the all of creation
Remember me as
Pablo Neruda

Dear Life,

First I must simply say Good Morning.
I would attempt to greet you this fine day
In all the languages I know
Or could 'Google',
But I already know
That you know them all
So please,
Once again
Forgive my laziness,
As you have done
For so many years now.

I meant to begin this letter
With offering my sincere gratitude
For yet another day
Where I may reverently greet you
And acknowledge this gift
You have allowed me to partake,
Life ...
Yet once again,
However,
My words and supposed wittyness
Got in the way
Of my heart-felt intent

Now, this letter-poem
Was not meant to be a
Confessional, but
There as always are
Many heavy burdens
Such as the guilt
Of indifference and apathy
That I silently bear

Each day,
And today,
This wonderful day
My soul definitively requires me
To speak on it.

To begin,
I realize,
Without a doubt that
I could have been
A better Son,
A better Brother,
A better Husband, Mate
A better Father
And a better Friend ...
Why hell, I could have been
A better Human-being,
And so much more!

You are also well aware that
I said many things
I should not have;
Kept silent when
I should have spoken out.
I did many things of which
I should have refrained,
And you and the Lorde knows
There are a myriad,
An abundance of things
I should have done ....
I apologize,
As I have done
So many times before.

Dear Life,
I earnestly wish for you to know
That these words are not empty,
But every once in a while
I am overcome
With this need
To dump all of me,
My foibles,
My errancies,
My weaknesses
Back upon You,
The Universe
And all of Creation ....
I only hope that once again
Forgiveness can be found
In your heart
Yet another day
For my infirmities.
....

Dear Life,
While I am at it,
Unloading my burdens
Into the ether,
I would be amiss
If I did not speak
To the other side of the coin,
You, 'Life' has graciously
Bestowed upon me.
.....

I wish to thank 'You' for all
Th precious moments
I have ever exerienced
During this journey,
At least the ones I can remember,
And I must say,
I humbly thank you

For the ones
I can not.

.....

I do realize that each
Of these life glimpses
And experiences
Have shaped and molded me
To become the man,
The person,
The Human-being
Who now reverntly sits before you
To exact this confessional diatribe.

.....

Dear Life,
I must thank 'You'
With all that I am for
All the people of whom
You gifted me the opportunity
To ingratiate my self with ...
Though not all of those experiences
Felt good during the times
Of happenings,
But in my waning years
I do realize
That each encounter
Served a purpose....
There were many a lesson
I did not understand then,
And i must confess,
Some do still yet
Escape me. ....
But I am trying ...
Some of the time.

.....

Let me let you know this,
I am so grateful that
After all these years
That my mind still says 'YES',
Though my body may dissent,
But thank you just the same.

And finally ...
As they say,
The first shall be the last,
And
The last shall be the first ..
.....
I want to thank you for
FAMILY ...,
Parents and Grands,
Aunts and Uncles,
My Ancestors
Who made a way for me.
I want to thank you for
My siblings,
My cousins, nieces and nephews
And the many others
Whom I claim as 'family'.

And lastly but definitely not least,
I must pay my obesance
For the greatest grace
Thou sought fit
To bestow upon
This needy soul;
And that is for
The gift of my seed, my children,
And the seed of my seed,
Ad infinitum,

For with this,
I have become a
'King in the Garden',
Your garden,
And I can never
Thank you enough . . . . .
Dear Life.

Thank you for all the smiles,
"Tears and Laughter"

The Spirit Speaks

I am but a 'Freedom Fighter'
Championing the rights of sovereignty.

I stand not alone
In this wilderness
Offering to the heavens
My thoughts, my words, my poems and my prose
Telling the story
Characterizing our plight,
Your plight
To our world

I am a rebel they say,
I say I am but a man
Whose spirit is troubled
By the times
We are given to endure

O dear 'Liberation',
Come unto to my people
And lift this oppressive hand
From our shoulders . . .

Let us find 'Righteousness'
Let us all collect, come together
For the good of one,
The good of all

May who I am
Be embraced by the heavens
And my offerings
Be a beacon of light

In this darkness,
And rise up, rise up
And shower themselves
The blessings of compassion
Upon the world of us all

July

2024

Featured Poets

~ * ~

Barbara Anna Gaiardoni

Bharati Nayak

Errol Bean

Michael Lee Johnson

i Fly
because
... said the Dreamer to the world.
I Can

www.iamjustbill.com

Barbara Anna Gaiardoni

Barbara Anna Gaiardoni is winner of the First Prize 2023 "Zheng Nian Cup" National Literature Price and finalist of the Edinburgh "Writings Leith" contest.

She receveid two nominations for the Touchstone Award 2023 and recognized on the Haiku Euro Top 100 list for 2023.

Her Japanese-style poems has been published in The Mainichi, Asahi Haikuist Network, The Japan Society UK and in one hundred and twenty other international journals. Drawing, swimmer and walking in nature are her passions. *"I can, I must, I will do it" her motto.*

http://barbaragaiardoni.altervista.org/blog/haikuco-2/

a cold
summer drink
in one hand
she smiles lost
in a memory

*

to dance the night
away barefoot
on the sand
the moon
turning red

*

the sea
smooths out
the farther
there's no use
looking fierce now

Bharati Nayak

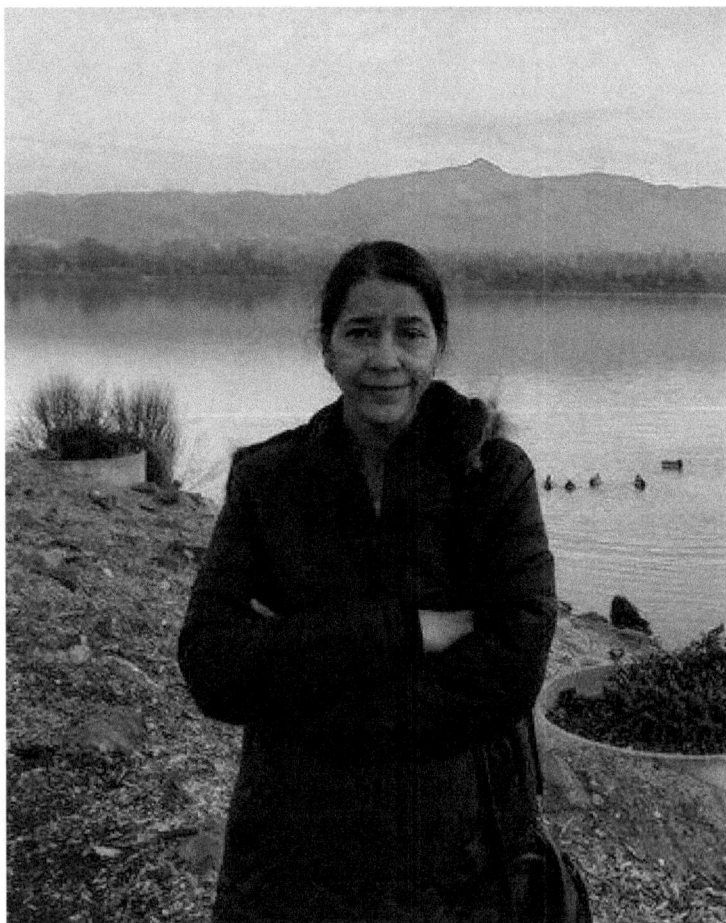

Bharati Nayak is a bilingual poet, writer ,editor and translator of India, writing in English and Odia. Her poems have been published in nearly 150 different magazines-zines ,anthologies ,books , e-books and newspapers of national and international repute such as Setumah Anthology, Inner Child Press, Amaravati Poetic Prismoids -Nova Literature, Circular Whispers, Cuckoo in Crisis, The Statesman and the like. She has published two poetry books in Odia, two English poetry collections as sole author ,six books in collaboration with different authors and translated Adiela Akoo's book 'Lost In A Quatrain ' into Odia .She has been felicitated at different literary forums .

Refugee

There were fury, fire, bombs and bullets
Army, terrorists, death and darkness
No water, no food, only deadly dance of death
They were leaving behind their dear homes and land
Leaving their cattle, dogs pets and food orchards
Their dreams shattered, they leave behind all treasure
They had no time to collect them, no means to carry them

Someone carrying his crippled son on his shoulder
Some one carrying his old father and a baby clinging to his mother
In their sunken eyes, fear writ large
To an unwelcome fate they march towards
Covering miles and miles through rough and tough terrains
Some jumping into ferry to escape death
But death encircling them from all sides
Death waiting them in black waters of sea
Orin hungry crocodile's teeth
Or in the congested refugee camp
In disease, hunger and thirst
Sometimes nature connives, when sun burns too hot
And wind blows too cold
Bereft of Home and Land
They gain only a name of pain
A refugee with a future uncertain
As a CIVILIZED SOCIETY with its stony heart just look
on.

If I can turn into a Poem

f I can turn into a Poem
I wish I could be your poem
The painted words of your art
The quietness of your poetry
And the softness of your words

I could be the fragrance
Drifting from your lines
I could be
The oceanic depth
Of philosophy
defining your poetry.

I could become
The soul of your quiet poem
That would ease
Each and every pain

I could be the
Decorated Chinese vessel
That would store
The beauty
Of your poetic wine.

I could be that poem of yours
That would need no words
And would become
The threshold to silence

I could be the zephyr wind
That would softly disperse
The sadness of things.

Bharati Nayak

If I could be
The voice of your poetry
That would become everyone's voice
And it would
Become the beating
Of a common heart.

From a poem
I would turn into poetry
That would reside
As the light
Of common soul.

A thousand miles away

A thousand miles away
George Floyd died
Of police brutality
His last words
Resonate here,
In my country
In my drawing room
In personal discussions
On T.V. and in newspapers
In breathless debates
Within protests and movements.

Why?
Because it is a rage of hundreds of years
Pressed under a knee
A simmering fire
That was waiting to conflagrate
A restless smoke
Suffocating people for years.

Was it a single man's murder?
No,
The way the brute police officer
Pressed his knee
On the neck of an unarmed black man
Was to show his power
To crush Floyd
Like a worthless being -
Not caring a damn
About his life.

The manner
In which the other police officers
Stood by
Showed how callous, how ruthless
They were, not caring a bit
When an innocent black man was dying.

'I can't breathe, I can't breathe'
The last words of Floyd
Resonate in every corner of our world
Questioning
The sanity of humankind.

Errol
Bean

Errol Bean

Errol D. Bean, a Jamaican author of two self-published books: *'A Flower Blooms'* (1998), an anthology of poems; *'Cynthia Schloss An Inspiration of Love and Friendship'* (2001), and a pending publication. Bean has recorded and released a number of gospel and conscious music. A graduate of United Theological College of the West Indies, University of the West Indies, School of Education (UWI), Bean has served as pastor, lecturer, life underwriter, marketing and communications manager. Married to Gloria, he is the proud father of one daughter, Dr. Dalea Bean. *Mantra: "To inspire and give hope to humanity through inspirational words.*

Lament of a Faded Flower
(A metaphor of a despondent woman)

Reminiscing –
No keen popping eyes, observing.
No curious, timid fingers, touching.
Gone forever, the tickling –
"Ohs", "Ahhs", "wows",
"m…m", "gosh", and "my, my" –
Dead are pleasant questions:
"Isn't this beautiful?"
"This is nice and cute, isn't it?"
Gone in the wind – "Exotic", "gorgeous".
Absent are gentle commands –
"Look at this."
"This you have to see."
No welcome demands –
"What is the name of this?"
"Where is it from?"
"Under what conditions does it thrive?"
"Does it like a lot of water?"
"What is the cost of this?"
I loathe this state,
this common malaise, I now share.
Here we are, drawn together for
contrast to enhance each
other, a mixed fragrance.
Look at me, who dreamed of
walking with a nervous, happy bride,
or waiting with an anxious groom!
I dreamed of approaching a closed
door and waiting for a pleasant
approving smile from a happy heart.
I dreamed of young, ready and vibrant,
(and soon over the hill or on the shelf)

spinsters tumbling, unabashed, in the
air to catch me in hope.
But here I am, surrounded by
others, stiff to their skeletons,
pretending strength,
savouring the last sip of life;
systems failing, limp, brown,
once green, bright and sure.
I, yesterday, a beautiful crown,
sat on erect spine, loosely in replenished
 water, anchored in crockery
– a life supporting well,
and a whiff of cheer I sent as willing
hands pulled me closer and revelled in my
delightful fragrance – but today
I peer through closing eyes;
I hear steps, yesterday staccato,
today a deadly diminuendo!
Sour wings fan the still air
and sing "farewell" – a tedium of death.
This is my hour – my glory, one by one,
falls into water, others on the place once
the pedestal, my elevation, now my refuse heap.
I see the corner of a pitiless eye.
In thought, it seems, "you have served your purpose.
Make way for the young, bright and strong."
(Oh God! ...
Is this the end for me?
Is there any hope for me?)
A vicious hand…
Together,
To the dump...

My Tears of Peace and Joy

It's strange; as a child,
I would cry when a young chicken
stepped on my foot or mashed my toe,
but as a grown man
I don't cry for my own physical pain
even when like torrent showers of rain
pain comes my way again and again…

I may groan, sigh and pray to heal
when my own excruciating pain I feel
but I cry not, matters not what's the source
of my pain, because when vibrations of real love
and tender care I get,
my grateful eyes always get wet.

I don't cry for my own pain
but when I'm whipped up by kindness
an attitude of heartical gratitude
triggers many a grateful tear
that mingle with the smile I wear.

I don't cry for my own pain
but my tears are ever so near
in moments of tranquil meditation,
when in deep fellowship with the Most High
sweet divine peace sweep over my soul,
and the strength of tender joy appears.

So, if you ever see my tear,
grieve not for me, have no fear,
may be am deeply touched by someone's
pain, or moved by their sorrow;

perhaps am empathising because of
the broken heart of someone I hold
close to my heart; some one that's
to me, is dear.

Yes, it may seem strange to see a grown man cry,
but never forget, it's not always what you see you'll get;
the tears you see in my eyes may seem bitter,
but please, be not on haste to muse, "he's bitter"
or blast it on **Twitter** – sorry, X;
the tears you see could just be tears of peace
that glitter in my eyes, and the joy of my God
warningly washing my face.

Seven Tips for a School Girl *

School girl, guard the door to your heart;
beware of "sweet" words of deception.
Heed the seven tips I give to you; write
them upon the lintels of your heart and
 the sons of deception shall depart.

Tip 1
Before you open your heart and give accommodation,
be head-smart and pay full attention;
learn the difference between love and infatuation, and
distinguish between genuine and imitation.

Tip 2
Examine their lines of communication - -
their aim is to disconnect your source of inspiration,
derail your education and your graduation
then relegate you to a life of degradation.

Tip 3
They will flatter you with disarming admiration;
shower you with enticing adoration;
surround you with "love" and sweet affection, and
make your eyes twinkle with fascination.

Tip 4
Then as you glory in this "elevation",
they break through your seal of protection!
Your mind, set on to pleasurable expectations,
you lose your focus and your concentration.

Tip 5
Next, they boggle your mind with the need for liberation;
remind you that you are the now generation!
Convince you to reject your parents' old-fashioned conversation.
Soon your personality undergoes a strange transformation.

Tip 6
Then you'll begin to act without contemplation,
and do things beyond your wildest imagination;
you become blind to your rapid degeneration
into a muddle of emotional complication!

Tip 7
So, to avoid the trap of deception,
simply look inward for self-affirmation;
steadfastly cling to your moral resolution,
and make your education your driving motivation.

* *Not a presumption that everyone who expresses an interest in "schoolgirls" sets out to deceive and exploit them; there are stories about schoolmates who formed meaningful, life-long relationships - - some culminating in successful marriages.*

Errol Bean

Michael Lee Johnson

Michael Lee Johnson

Michael Lee Johnson lived ten years in Canada during the Vietnam era. Today he is a poet in the greater Chicagoland area, IL. He has 300 YouTube poetry videos. Michael Lee Johnson is an internationally published poet in 45 countries, a song lyricist, has several published poetry books, has been nominated for 7 Pushcart Prize awards, and 6 Best of the Net nominations. He is editor-in-chief of 3 poetry anthologies, all available on Amazon, and has several poetry books and chapbooks. He has over 453 published poems. Michael is the administrator of 6 Facebook Poetry groups. Member Illinois State Poetry Society:

http://www.illinoispoets.org/.

Remember to consider me for Best of the Net or Pushcart nomination!

Ghost I Am

Here is a private hut
staring at me,
twigs & branches
over the top—
naked & alone.
I respond to an old 60s doo-wop
song: In the Still of the Night
Fred Parris and The Satins.

Storms are written in narratives,
old ears closed to a full hearing.
I'm but a shelter cringing.
In age, nightmare pre-warned redemption.
Let's call it the Jesus factor,
not LGBT symbols in Biden's world.
I lost my way close to the end.
Here is this shelter in heaven
poetry imagined spaces
prematurely still not all the words fit,
in childhood in abuse
lack of reason for bruises
rough hills, carp that didn't bite,
and Schwinn bike rides
flat tires, chains fall off, spokes collapse—
this thunder, those storms.

Find me a thumbnail
image of myself in centuries of dust.
Stand weakened by nature
of change glossed over, sealed.
Archives.
Old men, like a luxurious battery,
die hard, but with years, they
too, fade away.

California Summer

Coastal warm breeze

off Santa Monica, California

the sun turns salt

shaker upside down

and it rains white smog, a humid mist.

No thunder, no lightening,

nothing else to do

except for sashay

forward into liquid

and swim

into eternal days

like this.

Four Leaf Clover

I found your life smiling
inside a four-leaf clover.
Here you hibernate in sin.
You were dancing in the orange fields of the sun.
You lock into your history, your past, withdrawal,
taste honeycomb, then cow salt lick.
All your life, you have danced in your soft shoes.
Find free lottery tickets in the pockets of poor men and
strangers.
Numbers rhyme like winners, but they are just losers.
Positive numbers tug like gray blankets, poor horses
coming in 1st.
Private angry walls; desperate is the night.
You control intellect, josser men.
You take them in, push them out,
circle them with silliness.
Everything turns indigo blue in grief.
I hear your voice, fragmented words in thunder.
An actress buried in degrees of lousy weather and
blindness.
I leave you alone, wander the prairie path by myself.
Pray for wildflowers, the simple types. No one cares.
Purple colors, false colors, hibiscus on guard,
lilacs are freedom seekers, now no howls in death.
You are the cookie crumble of my dreams.
Three marriages in the past.
I hear you knocking my walls down, heaven stars creating
dreams.
Once beautiful in the rainbow sun, my face, even snow
now cast in banners, blank, fire, and flames.
I cycle a self-absorbed nest of words.

Remembering

our fallen soldiers of verse

Janet Perkins Caldwell

February 14, 1959 ~ September 20, 2016

Alan W. Jankowski

16 March 1961 ~ 10 March 2017

The Butterfly Effect

"IS" in effect

Inner Child Press

News

Published Books

by

Poetry Posse Members

We are so excited to share and announce a few of the current books, as well as the new and upcoming books of some of our Poetry Posse authors.

On the following pages we present to you ...

Alicja Maria Kuberska

Jackie Davis Allen

Gail Weston Shazor

hülya n. yılmaz

Nizar Sartawi

Elizabeth E. Castillo

Faleeha Hassan

Fahredin Shehu

Kimberly Burnham

Caroline 'Ceri' Nazareno

Eliza Segiet

Teresa E. Gallion

Mutawaf Shaheed

William S. Peters, Sr.

Now Available

www.innerchildpress.com

I Am in Your Head

C. E. Shy

Now Available
www.innerchildpress.com

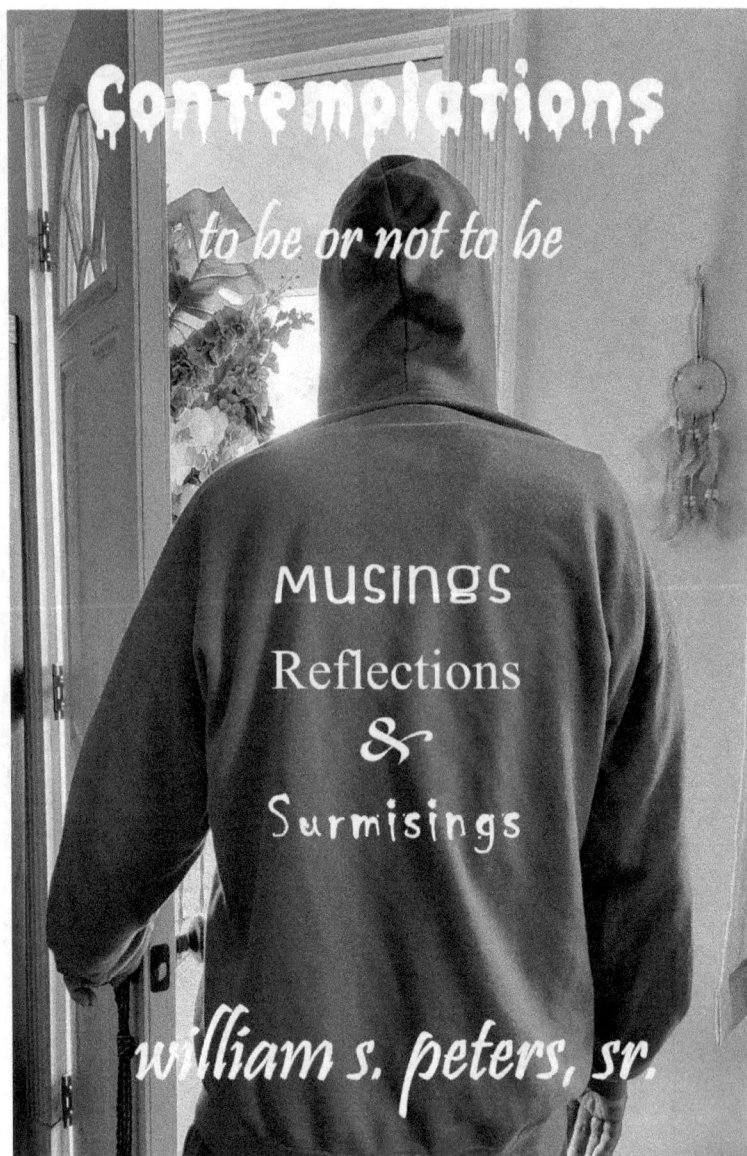

Contemplations

to be or not to be

musings
Reflections
&
Surmisings

william s. peters, sr.

Now Available
www.innerchildpress.com

Come Egypt

Poetry by

Teresa E. Gallion

Now Available
www.innerchildpress.com

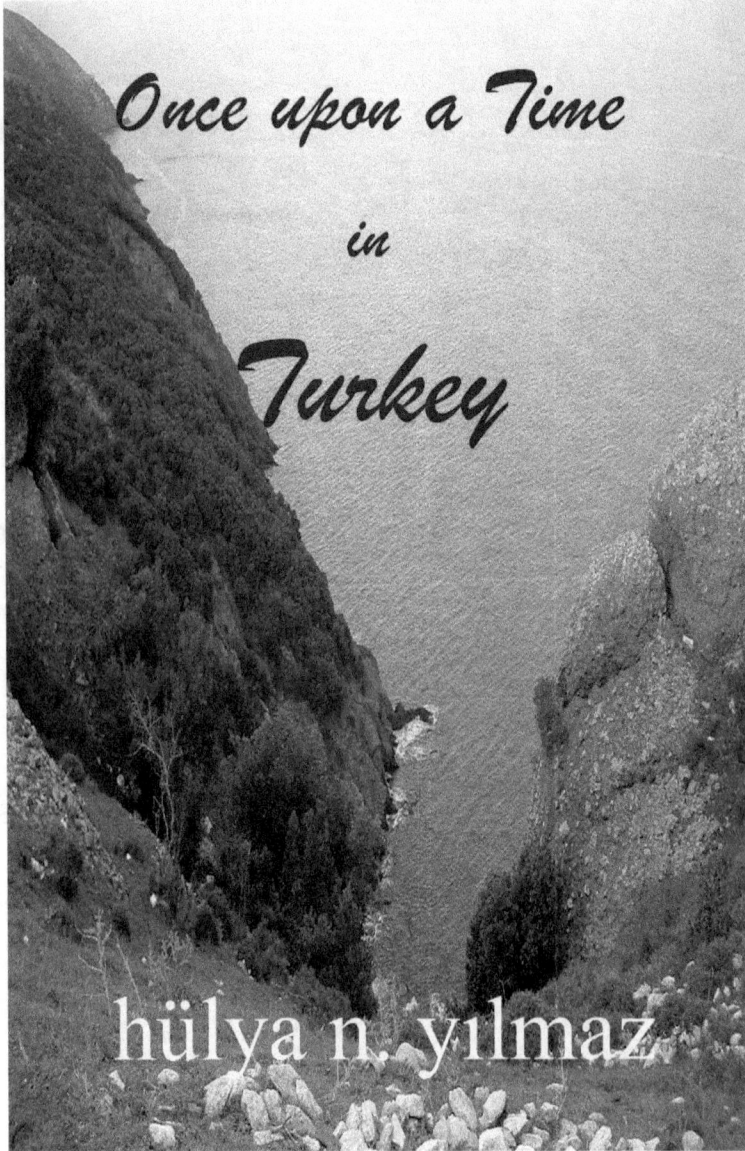

Once upon a Time

in

Turkey

hülya n. yılmaz

Now Available
www.innerchildpress.com

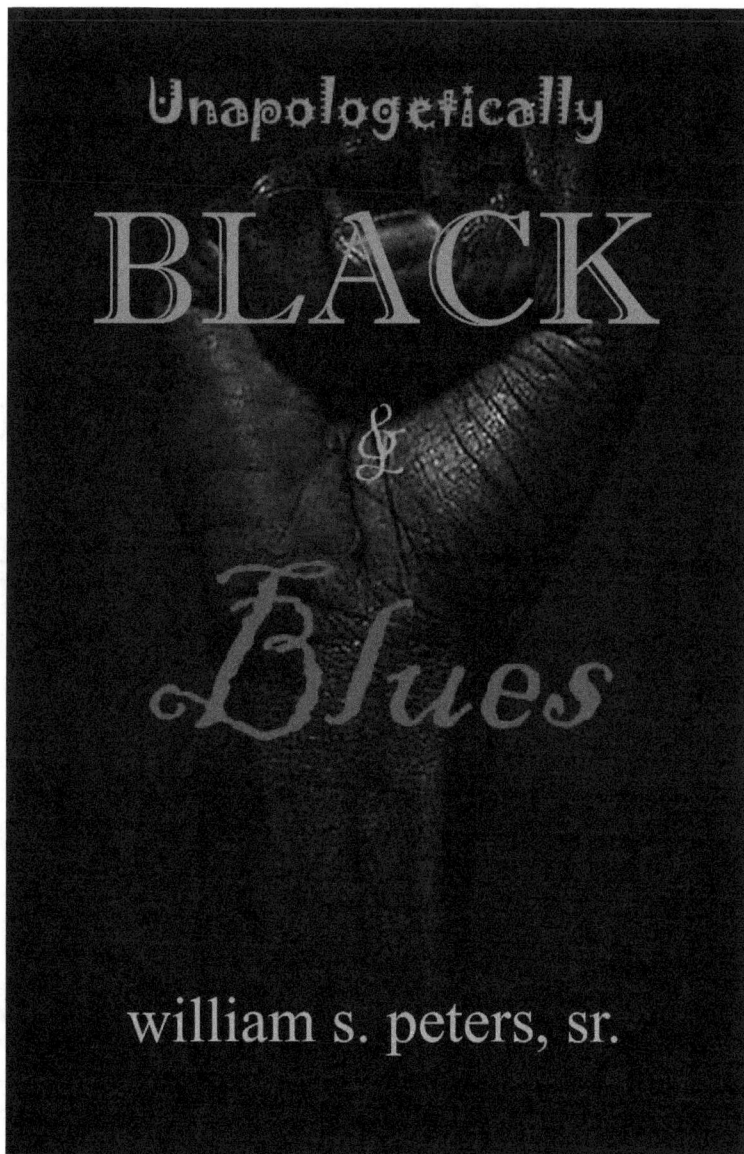

Unapologetically
BLACK
&
Blues

william s. peters, sr.

Now Available
www.innerchildpress.com

Pulling Coats

Shareef Abdur-Rasheed

Now Available
www.innerchildpress.com

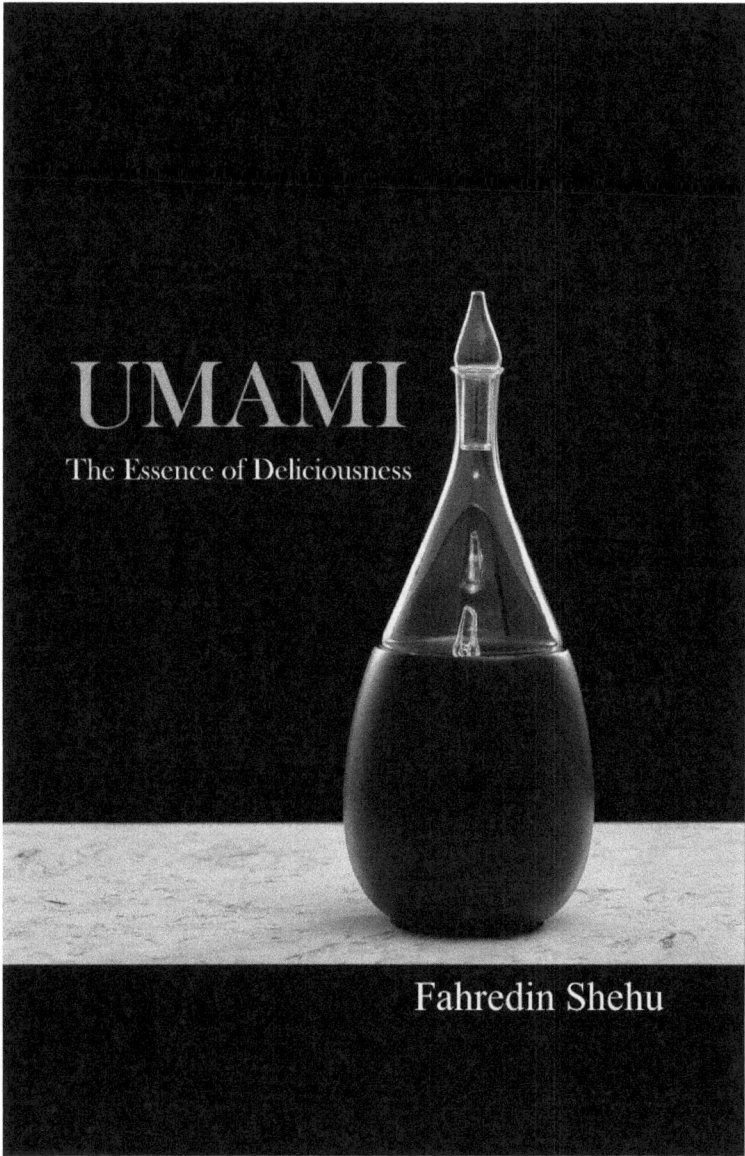

Now Available

www.innerchildpress.com

After the Frost

Alicja Maria Kuberska

Now Available
www.innerchildpress.com

Fahredin Shehu

ORMUS

Now Available

www.innerchildpress.com

Ahead of My Time

...from the Streets to the Stages

Albert 'Infinite' Carrasco

Now Available

www.innerchildpress.com

Eliza Segiet

To Be More

Now Available at
www.innerchildpress.com

SEARCH FOR THE MAGICAL MULTILINGUAL FROG

A Tale of Ribbit in 50 Languages

KIMBERLY BURNHAM

Now Available at

www.amazon.com/gp/product/B08MYL5B7S/ref=
dbs_a_def_rwt_hsch_vapi_tkin_p1_i2

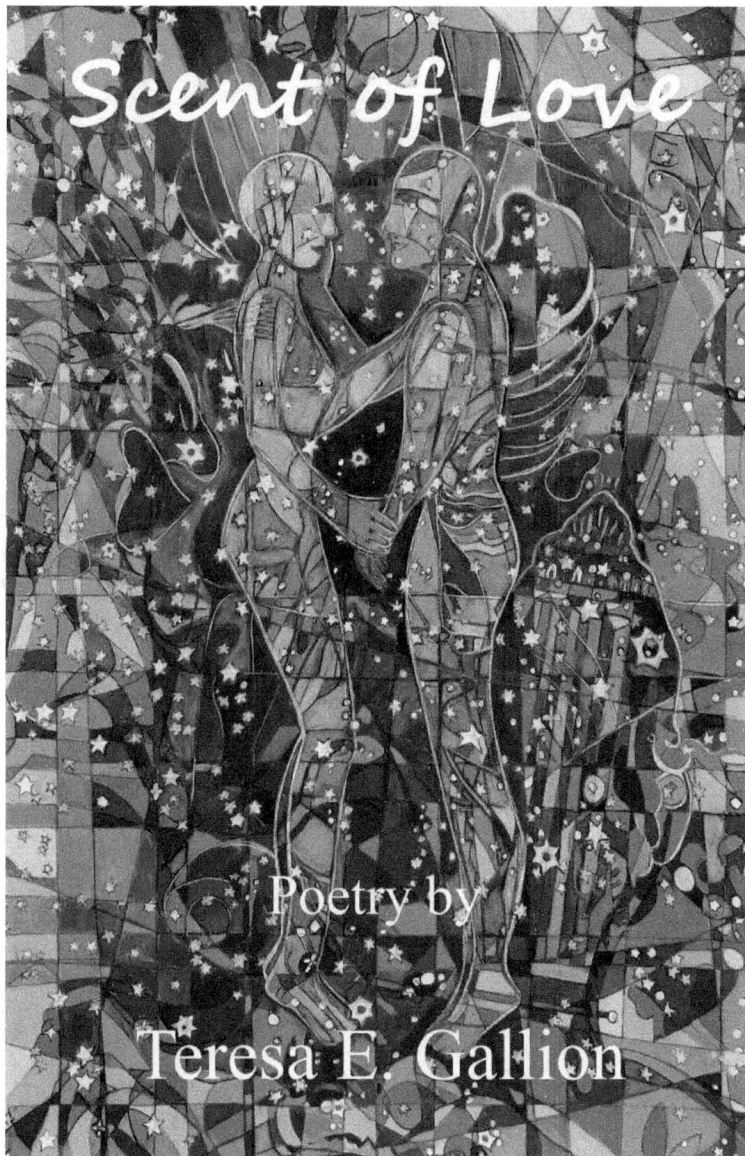

Scent of Love

Poetry by

Teresa E. Gallion

Now Available

www.innerchildpress.com

Inner Reflections
of the
Muse

Elizabeth Castillo

Now Available

www.innerchildpress.com

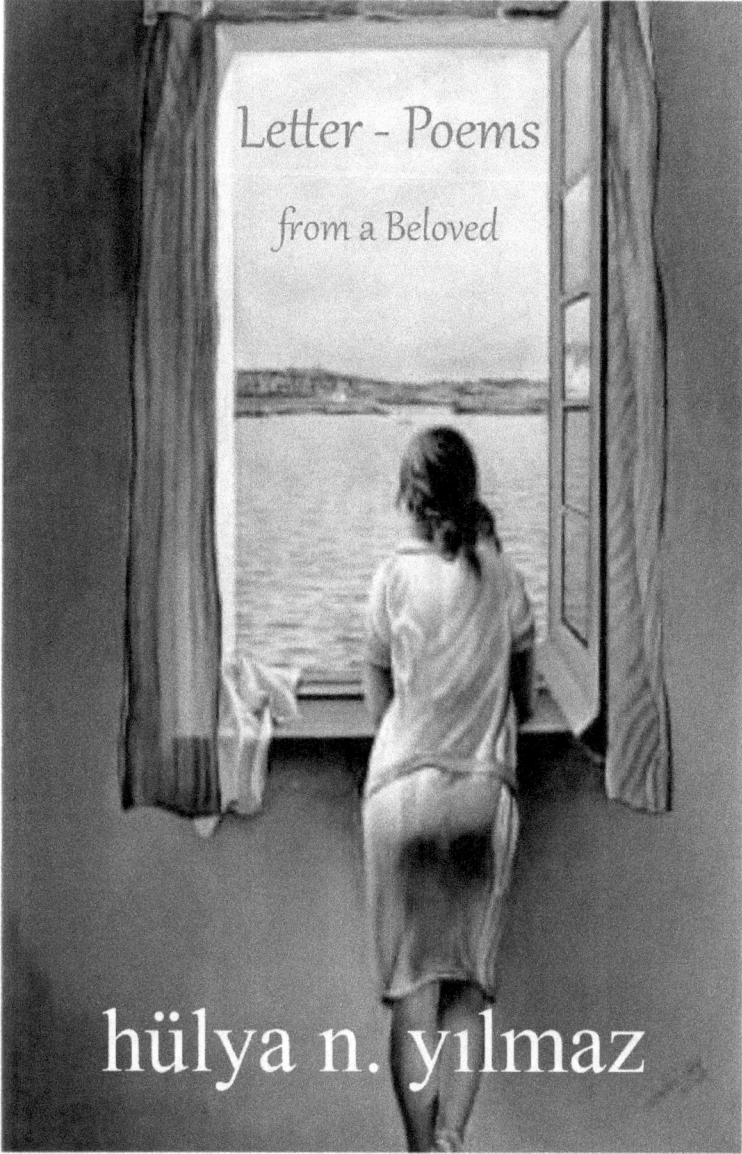

Letter - Poems

from a Beloved

hülya n. yılmaz

Now Available

www.innerchildpress.com

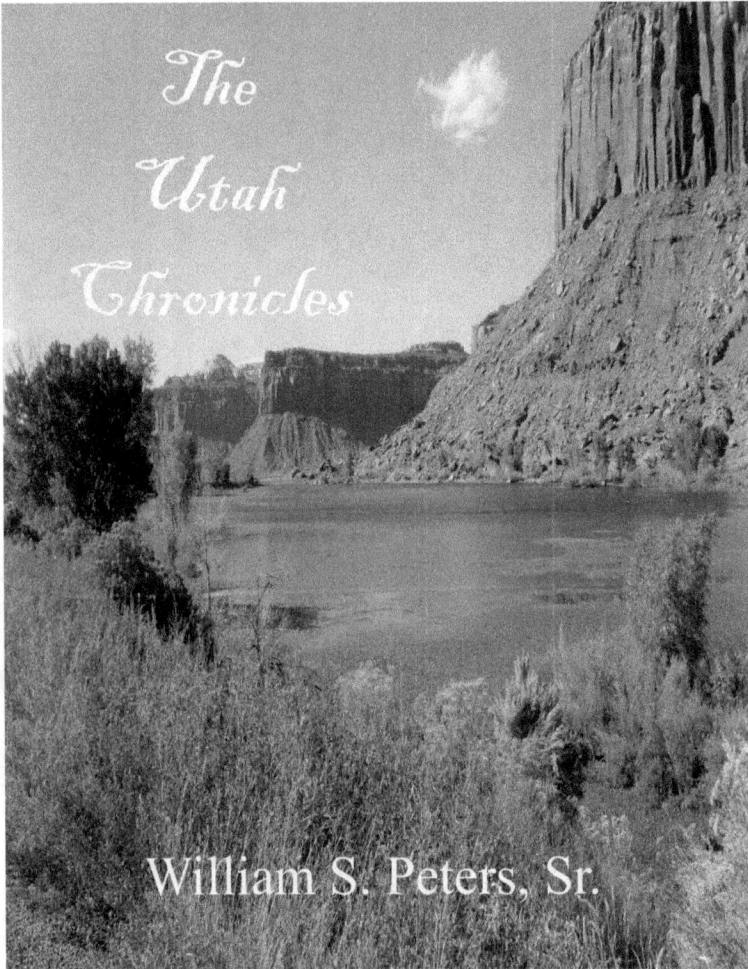

The Utah Chronicles

William S. Peters, Sr.

Now Available

www.innerchildpress.com

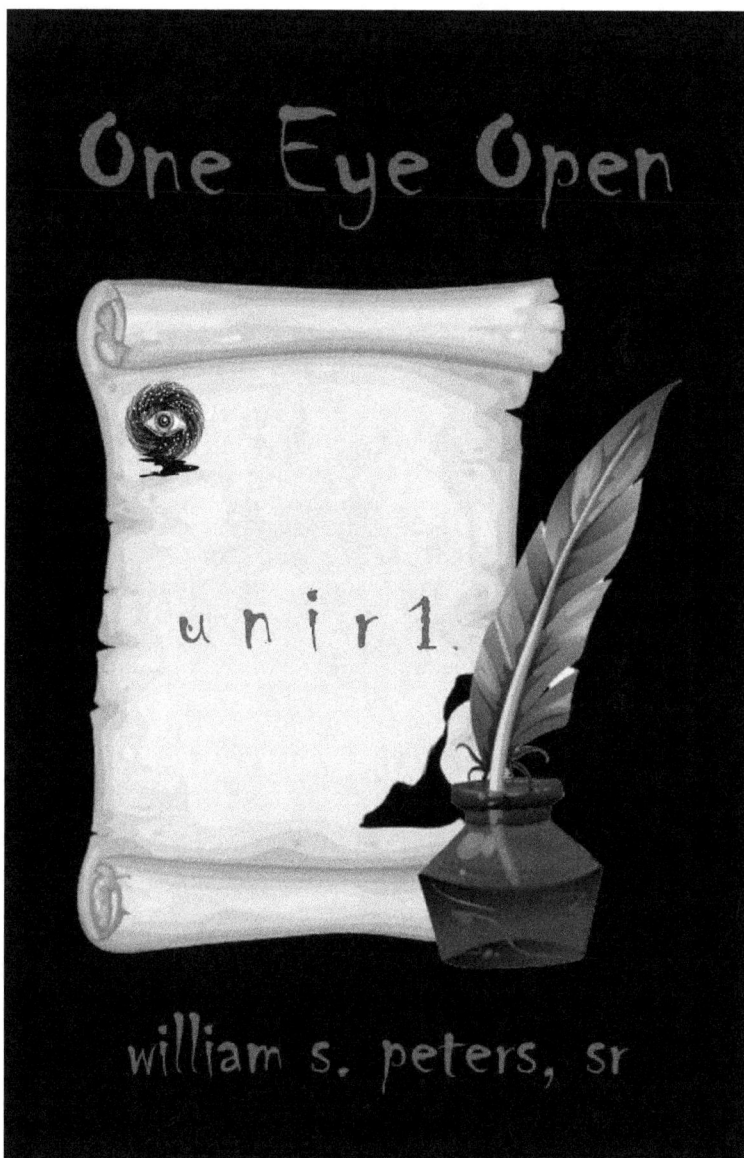

One Eye Open

u n i r 1.

william s. peters, sr

Now Available

www.innerchildpress.com

The Book of krisar

volume v

william s. peters, sr.

Now Available

www.innerchildpress.com

The Book of krisar

Volume I

william s. peters, sr.

The Book of krisar

Volume II

william s. peters, sr.

Now Available

www.innerchildpress.com

The Book of krisar

Volume III

william s. peters, sr.

The Book of krisar

Volume IV

william s. peters, sr.

Now Available

www.innerchildpress.com

Velvet Passions

of

Calibrated Quarks

Caroline Nazareno-Gabis

Now Available

www.innerchildpress.com

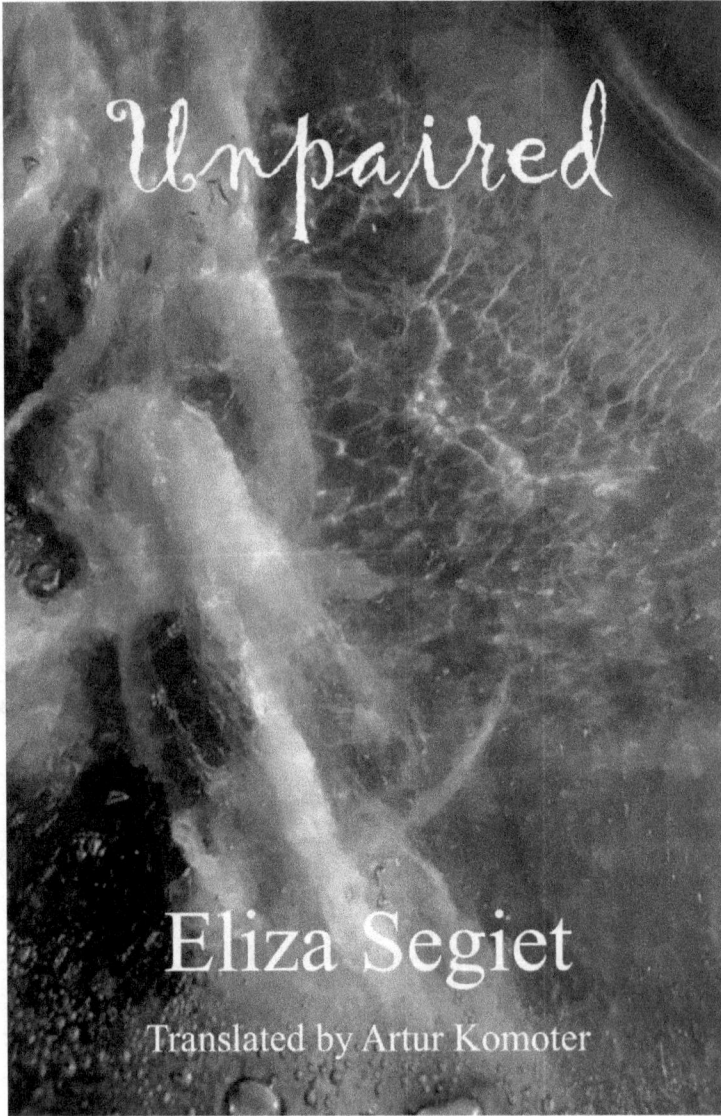

Unpaired

Eliza Segiet

Translated by Artur Komoter

Private Issue

www.innerchildpress.com

Canlarım

My Lifeblood

poetry in Turkish and English

hülya n. yılmaz

Now Available
www.innerchildpress.com

Butterfly's Voice

Faleeha Hassan

Translated by William M. Hutchins

Now Available at
www.innerchildpress.com

No Illusions

Through the Looking Glass

Jackie Davis Allen

Now Available at

www.innerchildpress.com

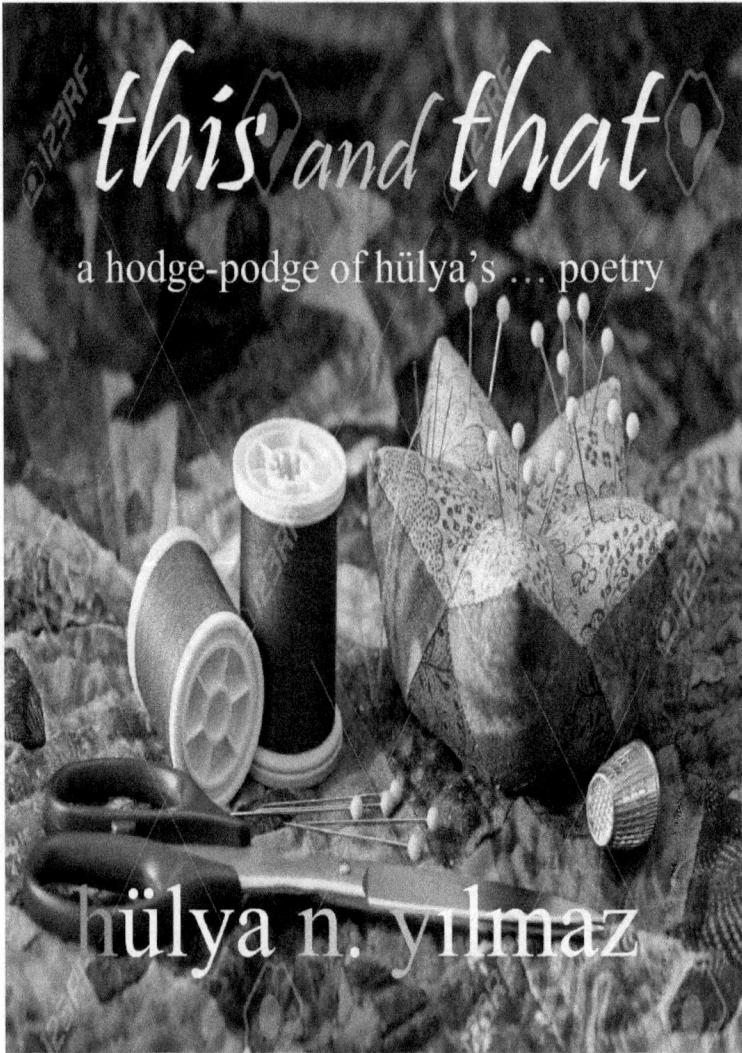

this and that

a hodge-podge of hülya's ... poetry

hülya n. yılmaz

Now Available at

www.innerchildpress.com

Eclectic Verse

mommy i hear those whispers . . . (again)

WilliAM s. PeTers, sR.

Now Available at
www.innerchildpress.com

HERENOW

FAHREDIN SHEHU

Now Available at
www.innerchildpress.com

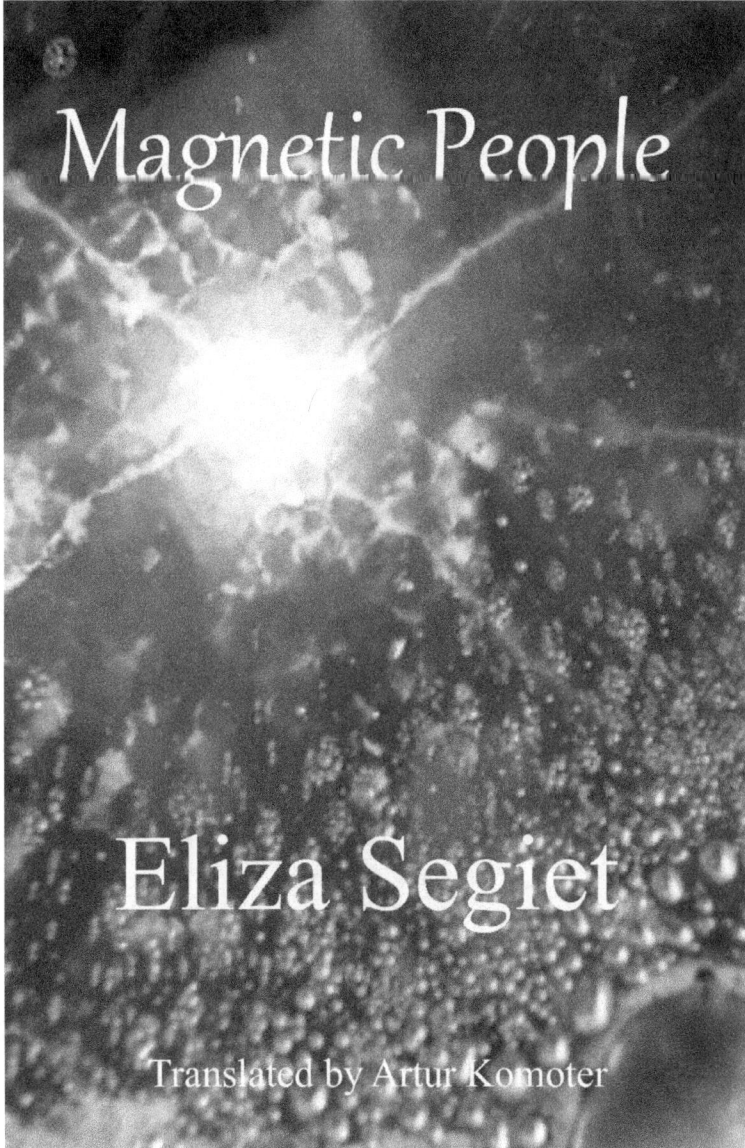

Magnetic People

Eliza Segiet

Translated by Artur Komoter

Now Available at
www.innerchildpress.com

Dark Side of the Moon

Jackie Davis Allen

Now Available at
www.innerchildpress.com

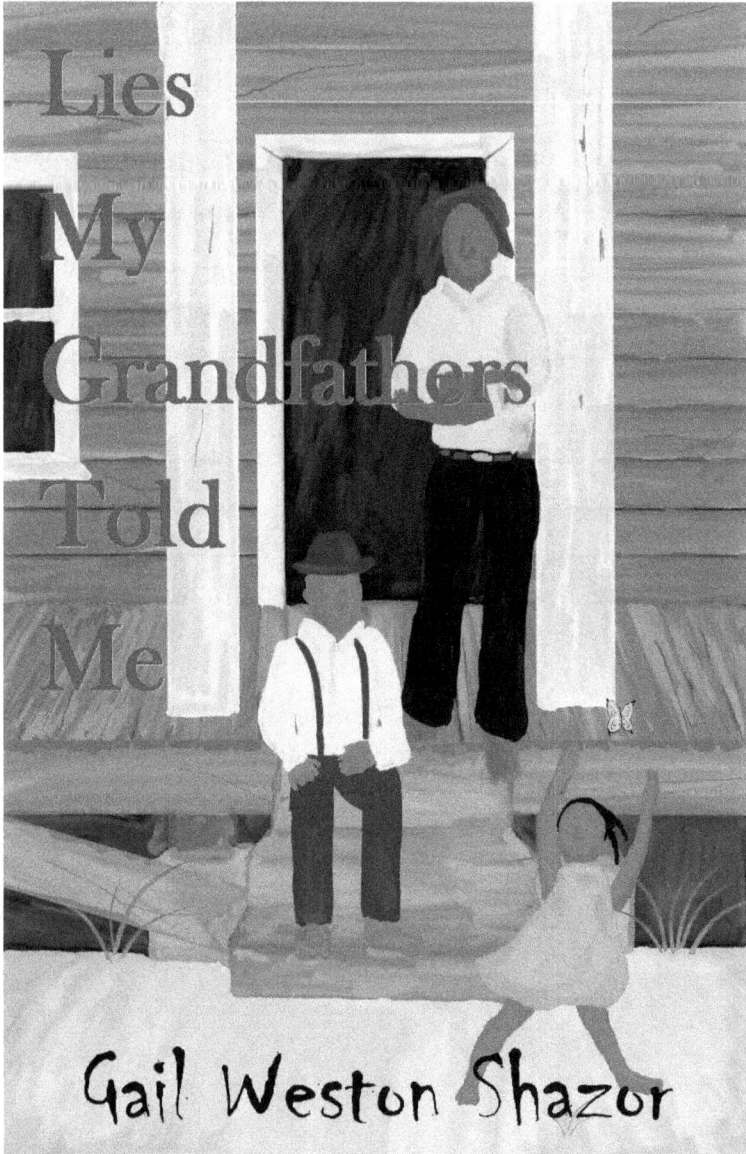

Lies
My
Grandfathers
Told
Me

Gail Weston Shazor

Now Available at
www.innerchildpress.com

Aflame

Memoirs in Verse

hülya n. yılmaz

Now Available at
www.innerchildpress.com

Mass Graves

Faleeha Hassan

Now Available at
www.innerchildpress.com

Breakfast

for

Butterflies

Faleeha Hassan

Now Available at
www.innerchildpress.com

7 Days
in
Palestine

william s. peters sr.

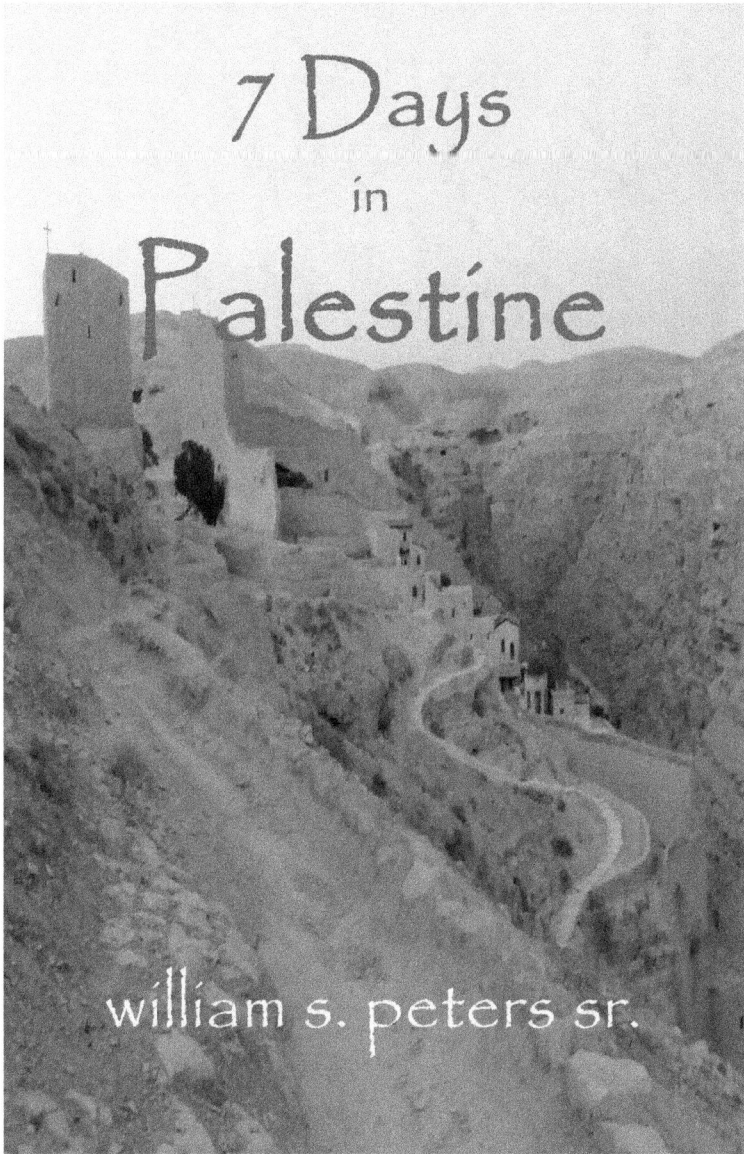

Now Available at
www.innerchildpress.com

inner child press
presents

Tunisian Dreams

william s. peters, sr.

Now Available at

www.innerchildpress.com

INNER CHILD PRESS

THIS IS WHY I
SLEEP

william s. peters sr.

Now Available at
www.innerchildpress.com

Other

Anthological

works from

Inner Child Press International

www.innerchildpress.com

Now Available

www.worldhealingworldpeacepoetry.com

Now Available

www.worldhealingworldpeacepoetry.com

World Healing
World Peace
2022

Poets for Humanity

Now Available

www.worldhealingworldpeacepoetry.com

World Healing World Peace
2020

Poets for Humanity

Now Available

www.worldhealingworldpeacepoetry.com

I want to
Live

an examination of Black & White issues

POETRY

ANALYSES

STORIES

CREATIVE WRITING

CRITICAL ESSAYS

WRITERS FOR HUMANITY

Now Available

www.innerchildpress.com

Inner Child Press International
&
The Year of the Poet
present

Poetry

the best of 2020

Poets of the World

Now Available
www.innerchildpress.com

Inner Child Press International

presents

W.A.R.

We Are Revolution

Poets for Humanity

Now Available
www.innerchildpress.com

the Heart of a Poet

words for a better tomorrow

The Conscious Poets

Now Available
www.innerchildpress.com

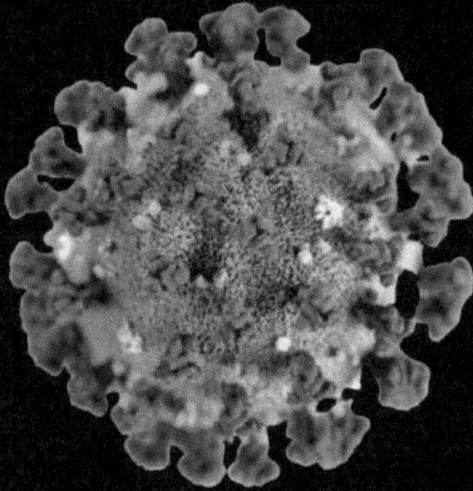

Corona

Social Distancing

Poets for Humanity

Now Available
www.innerchildpress.com

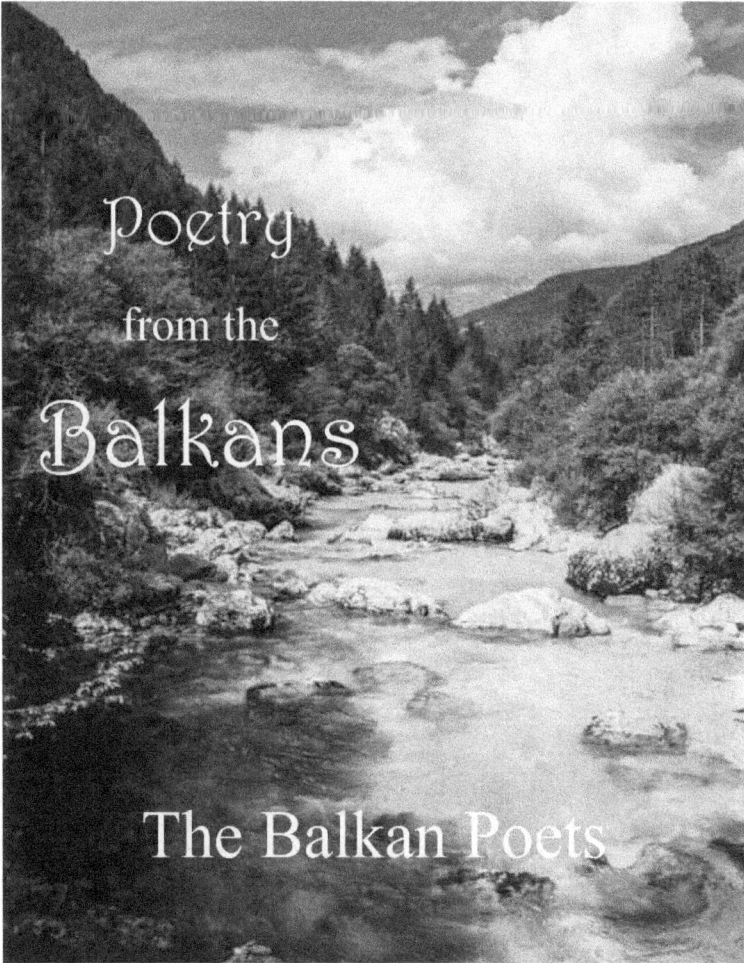

Poetry
from the
Balkans

The Balkan Poets

Now Available at
www.innerchildpress.com

Now Available at
www.innerchildpress.com

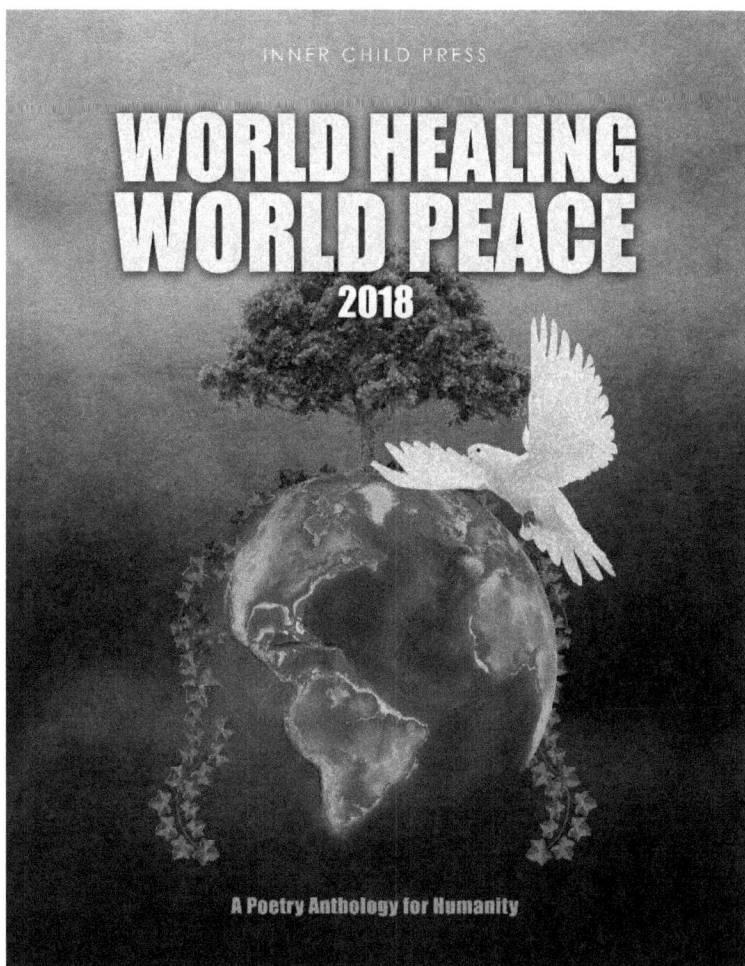

Now Available at
www.innerchildpress.com

Inner Child Press International
presents

A Love Anthology

2019

The Love Poets

Now Available

www.worldhealingworldpeacepoetry.com

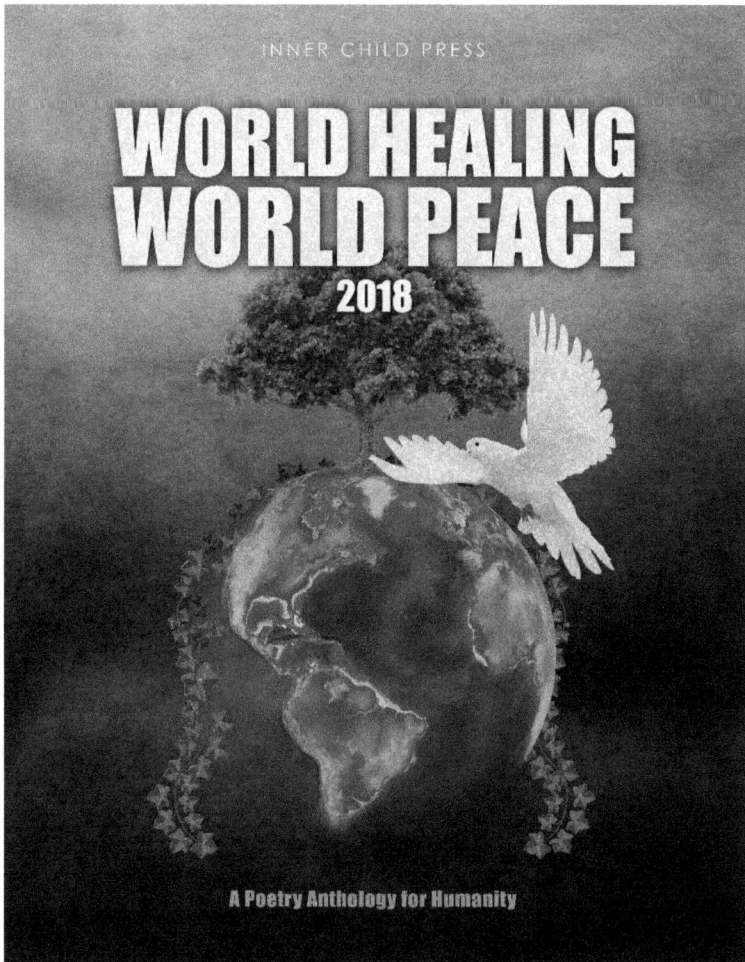

INNER CHILD PRESS

WORLD HEALING WORLD PEACE
2018

A Poetry Anthology for Humanity

Now Available
www.worldhealingworldpeacepoetry.com

World Healing World Peace
INNER CHILD PRESS
A Poetry Anthology 2014
Volume 1

World Healing World Peace
INNER CHILD PRESS
A Poetry Anthology 2014
Volume 2

World Healing World Peace
A POETRY ANTHOLOGY
Volume 1

World Healing World Peace
A POETRY ANTHOLOGY
Volume 2

Now Available

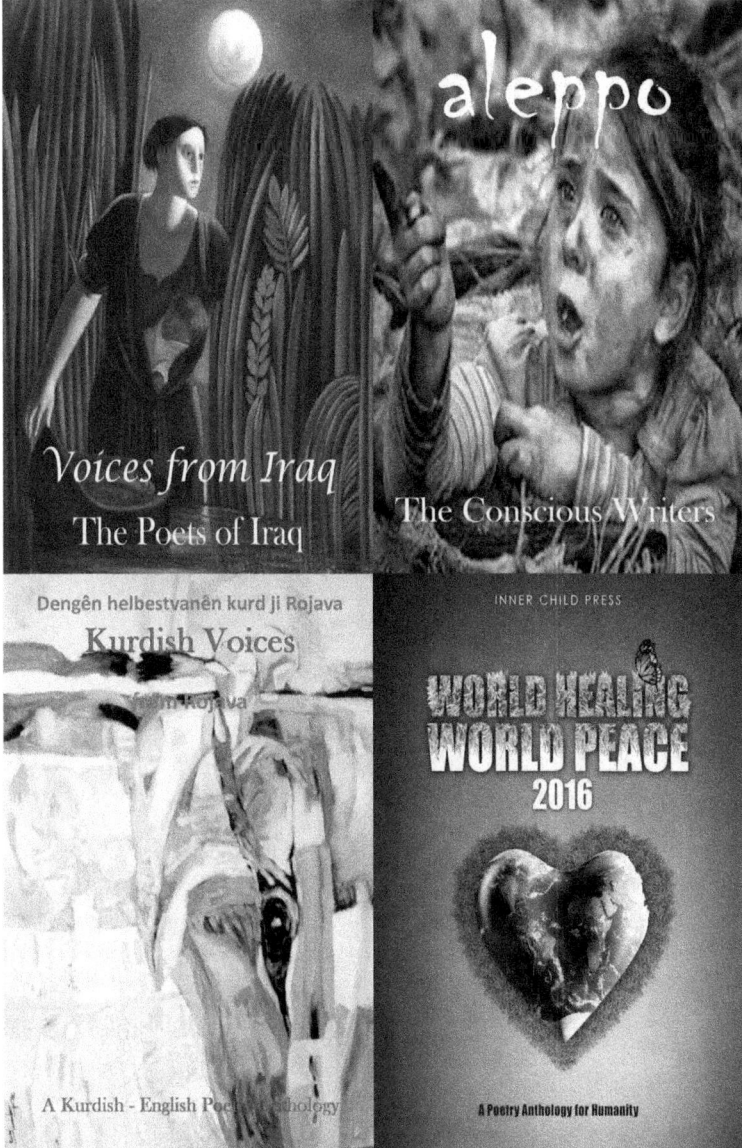

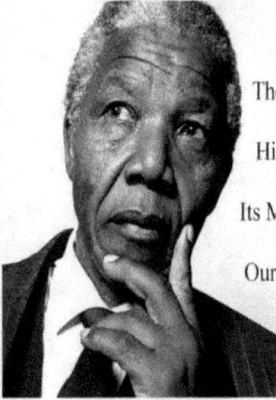

Mandela

The Man

His Life

Its Meaning

Our Words

Poetry . . . Commentary & Stories
The Anthological Writers

A GATHERING OF WORDS

POETRY & COMMENTARY
FOR
TRAYVON MARTIN

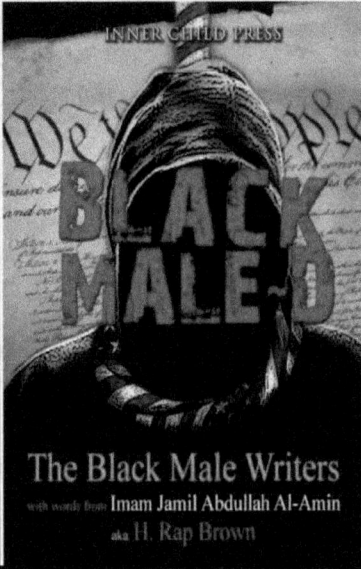

INNER CHILD PRESS

BLACK MALE~D

The Black Male Writers
with words from Imam Jamil Abdullah Al-Amin
aka H. Rap Brown

I want my poetry to... *volume* 4

the conscious poets

inspired by . . . Monte Smith

Now Available

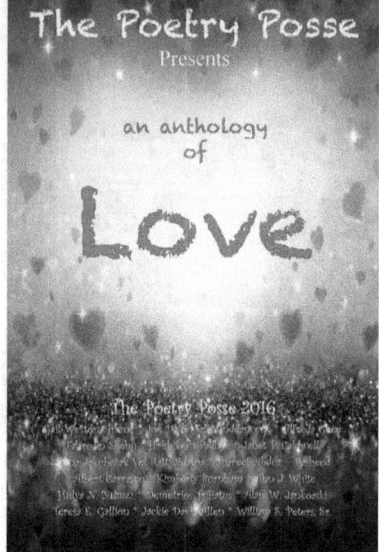

Now Available

a collection of the Voices of Many inspired by . . .

Monte Smith

i want my PoEtRy to . . .

a collection of the Voices of Many inspired by . . .

Monte Smith

i want my PoEtRy to . . .

volume II

i want my PoEtRy to . . . volume 3

a collection of the Voices of Many inspired by . . .

Monte Smith

11 Words

(9 lines . . .)

for those who are challenged

an anthology of Poetry inspired by . . .

Poetry Dancer

Now Available

www.innerchildpress.com/anthologies

The Year of the Poet
January 2014

The Poetry Posse

Jamie Bond
Gail Weston Shazor
Albert 'Infinite' Carrasco
Siddartha Beth Pierce
Janet P. Caldwell
June 'Bugg' Barefield
Debbie M. Allen
Tony Henninger
Joe DaVerbal Minddancer
Robert Gibbons
Neetu Wali
Shareef Abdur-Rasheed
William S. Peters, Sr.

Carnation

Our January Feature
Terri L. Johnson

the Year of the Poet

February 2014

violets

The Poetry Posse

Jamie Bond
Gail Weston Shazor
Albert 'Infinite' Carrasco
Siddartha Beth Pierce
Janet P. Caldwell
June 'Bugg' Barefield
Debbie M. Allen
Tony Henninger
Joe DaVerbal Minddancer
Robert Gibbons
Neetu Wali
Shareef Abdur-Rasheed
William S. Peters, Sr.

Our February Features
Teresa E. Gallion & Robert Gibson

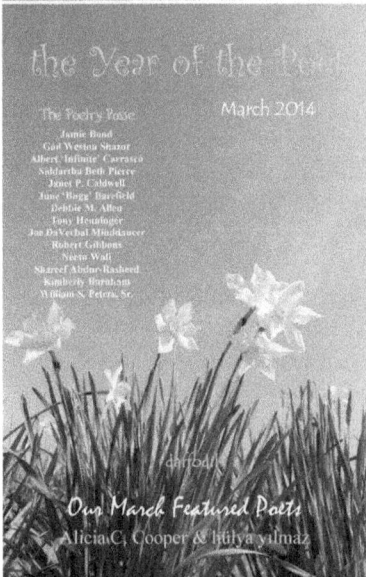

the Year of the Poet
March 2014

The Poetry Posse

Jamie Bond
Gail Weston Shazor
Albert 'Infinite' Carrasco
Siddartha Beth Pierce
Janet P. Caldwell
June 'Bugg' Barefield
Debbie M. Allen
Tony Henninger
Joe DaVerbal Minddancer
Robert Gibbons
Neetu Wali
Shareef Abdur-Rasheed
Kimberly Burnham
William S. Peters, Sr.

daffodil

Our March Featured Poets
Alicia C. Cooper & hülya yılmaz

the Year of the Poet

April 2014

The Poetry Posse

Jamie Bond
Gail Weston Shazor
Albert 'Infinite' Carrasco
Siddartha Beth Pierce
Janet P. Caldwell
June 'Bugg' Barefield
Debbie M. Allen
Tony Henninger
Joe DaVerbal Minddancer
Robert Gibbons
Neetu Wali
Shareef Abdur-Rasheed
Kimberly Burnham
William S. Peters, Sr.

Our April Featured Poets
Fahredin Shehu
Martina Reisz Newberry
Justin Blackburn
Monte Smith

Sweet Pea

celebrating international poetry month

Now Available
www.innerchildpress.com/the-year-of-the-poet

the year of the poet
May 2014

May's Featured Poets

RaaGaa
Joski the Poet
Shannon Stanton

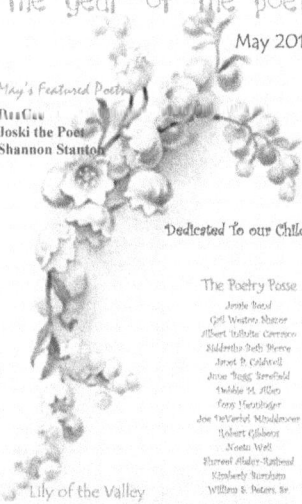

Dedicated to our Children

The Poetry Posse

Jamie Bond
Gail Weston Shazor
Albert Infinite Carrasco
Siddhartha Beth Pierce
Janet P. Caldwell
June Bugg Barefield
Debbie M. Allen
Tony Henninger
Joe DaVerbal Minddancer
Robert Gibbons
Neetu Wali
Shareef Abdur-Rasheed
Kimberly Burnham
William S. Peters, Sr.

Lily of the Valley

the Year of the Poet
June 2014

Love & Relationship

Rose

June's Featured Poets

Shantelle McLin
Jacqueline D. E. Kennedy
Abraham N. Benjamin

The Poetry Posse

Jamie Bond
Gail Weston Shazor
Albert Infinite' Carrasco
Siddartha Beth Pierce
Janet P. Caldwell
June Bugg Barefield
Debbie M. Allen
Tony Henninger
Joe DaVerbal Minddancer
Robert Gibbons
Neetu Wali
Shareef Abdur-Rasheed
Kimberly Burnham
William S. Peters, Sr.

The Year of the Poet
July 2014

July Feature Poets

Christena A. V. Williams
Dr. John R. Strum
Kolade Olanrewaju Freedom

The Poetry Posse

Jamie Bond
Gail Weston Shazor
Siddartha Beth Pierce
Janet P. Caldwell
June Bugg Barefield
Debbie M. Allen
Tony Henninger
Joe DaVerbal Minddancer
Robert Gibbons
Neetu Wali
Shareef Abdur-Rasheed
Kimberly Burnham
William S. Peters, Sr.

Lotus
Asian Flower of the Month

The Year of the Poet
August 2014

Gladiolus

The Poetry Posse

Jamie Bond
Gail Weston Shazor
Albert 'Infinite' Carrasco
Siddartha Beth Pierce
Janet P. Caldwell
June Bugg Barefield
Debbie M. Allen
Tony Henninger
Joe DaVerbal Minddancer
Robert Gibbons
Neetu Wali
Shareef Abdur-Rasheed
Kimberly Burnham
William S. Peters, Sr.

August Feature Poets

Ann White * Rosalind Cherry * Sheila Jerkins

Now Available

www.innerchildpress.com/the-year-of-the-poet

213

The Year of the Poet
September 2014
Aster — Morning-Glory
Wild Chicory September Birthday Flower
September Feature Poets
Florence Malone * Keith Alan Hamilton

The Poetry Posse
Jamie Bond * Gail Weston Shazor * Albert 'Infinite' Carrasco * Siddartha Beth Pierce
Janet P. Caldwell * June 'Bugg' Barefield * Debbie M. Allen * Tony Henninger
Joe DeVerbal Minddancer * Robert Gibbons * Neetu Wali * Shareef Abdur-Rasheed
Kimberly Burnham * William S. Peters, Sr.

THE YEAR OF THE POET
October 2014
Red Poppy

The Poetry Posse
Jamie Bond * Gail Weston Shazor * Albert 'Infinite' Carrasco * Siddartha Beth Pierce
Janet P. Caldwell * June 'Bugg' Barefield * Debbie M. Allen * Tony Henninger
Joe DeVerbal Minddancer * Robert Gibbons * Neetu Wali * Shareef Abdur-Rasheed
Kimberly Burnham * William S. Peters, Sr.

October Feature Poets
Ceri Naz * Rajendra Padhi * Elizabeth Castillo

THE YEAR OF THE POET
November 2014
Chrysanthemum

The Poetry Posse
Jamie Bond * Gail Weston Shazor * Albert 'Infinite' Carrasco * Siddartha Beth Pierce
Janet P. Caldwell * June 'Bugg' Barefield * Debbie M. Allen * Tony Henninger
Joe DeVerbal Minddancer * Robert Gibbons * Neetu Wali * Shareef Abdur-Rasheed
Kimberly Burnham * William S. Peters, Sr.

November Feature Poets
Jocelyn Mosman * Jackie Allen * James Moore * Neville Hiatt

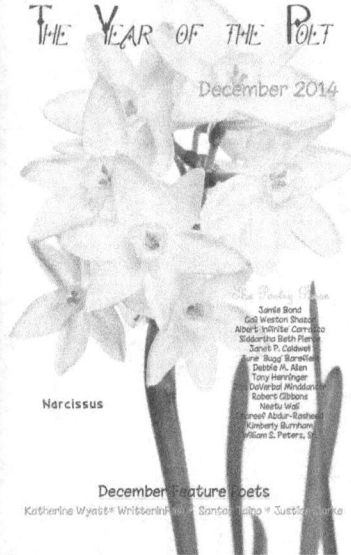

THE YEAR OF THE POET
December 2014
Narcissus

The Poetry Posse
Jamie Bond
Gail Weston Shazor
Albert 'Infinite' Carrasco
Siddartha Beth Pierce
Janet P. Caldwell
June 'Bugg' Barefield
Debbie M. Allen
Tony Henninger
DeVerbal Minddancer
Robert Gibbons
Neetu Wali
Shareef Abdur-Rasheed
Kimberly Burnham
William S. Peters, Sr.

December Feature Poets
Katherine Wyatt* WritterInPink * Santos Rubio * Justin Clarke

Now Available
www.innerchildpress.com/the-year-of-the-poet

THE YEAR OF THE POET II
January 2015

Garnet

The Poetry Posse

Jamie Bond
Gail Weston Shazor
Albert 'Infinite' Carrasco
Siddartha Beth Pierce
Janet P. Caldwell
Tony Henninger
Joe DaVerbal Minddancer
Robert Gibbons
Neetu Wali
Shareef Abdur – Rasheed
Kimberly Burnham
Ann White
Keith Alan Hamilton
Katherine Wyatt
Fahredin Shehu
Hülya N. Yılmaz
Teresa E. Gallion
Jackie Allen
William S. Peters, Sr.

January Feature Poets

Bismay Mohanti * Jen Walls * Eric Judah

THE YEAR OF THE POET ii
February 2015

Amethyst

THE POETRY POSSE

Jamie Bond
Gail Weston Shazor
Albert 'Infinite' Carrasco
Siddartha Beth Pierce
Janet P. Caldwell
Tony Henninger
Joe DaVerbal Minddancer
Robert Gibbons
Neetu Wali
Shareef Abdur – Rasheed
Kimberly Burnham
Ann White
Keith Alan Hamilton
Katherine Wyatt
Fahredin Shehu
Hülya N. Yılmaz
Teresa E. Gallion
Jackie Allen
William S. Peters, Sr.

FEBRUARY FEATURE POETS

Iram Fatima * Bob McNeil * Kerstin Centervall

The Year of the Poet II
March 2015

Our Featured Poets

Heung Sook * Anthony Arnold * Alicia Poland

Bloodstone

The Poetry Posse 2015

Jamie Bond * Gail Weston Shazor * Albert 'Infinite' Carrasco
Siddartha Beth Pierce * Janet P. Caldwell * Tony Henninger
Joe DaVerbal Minddancer * Neetu Wali * Shareef Abdur – Rasheed
Kimberly Burnham * Ann White * Keith Alan Hamilton
Katherine Wyatt * Fahredin Shehu * Hülya N. Yılmaz
Teresa E. Gallion * Jackie Allen * William S. Peters, Sr

The Year of the Poet II
April 2015

Celebrating International Poetry Month

Our Featured Poets

Raja Williams * Dennis Ferado * Laure Charazac

Diamonds

The Poetry Posse 2015

Jamie Bond * Gail Weston Shazor * Albert 'Infinite' Carrasco
Siddartha Beth Pierce * Janet P. Caldwell * Tony Henninger
Joe DaVerbal Minddancer * Neetu Wali * Shareef Abdur – Rasheed
Kimberly Burnham * Ann White * Keith Alan Hamilton
Katherine Wyatt * Fahredin Shehu * Hülya N. Yılmaz
Teresa E. Gallion * Jackie Allen * William S. Peters, Sr.

Now Available

www.innerchildpress.com/the-year-of-the-poet

The Year of the Poet II
May 2015

May's Featured Poets
Geri Algeri
Akin Mosi Chinnery
Anna Jakubcza...

Emeralds

The Poetry Posse 2015
Jamie Bond * Gail Weston Shazor * Albert 'Infinite' Carrasco
Siddartha Beth Pierce * Janet P. Caldwell * Tony Henninger
Joe DaVerbal Minddancer * Neetu Wali * Shareef Abdur – Rasheed
Kimberly Burnham * Ann White * Keith Alan Hamilton
Katherine Wyatt * Fahredin Shehu * Hülya N. Yılmaz
Teresa E. Gallion * Jackie Allen * William S. Peters, Sr.

The Year of the Poet II
June 2015

June's Featured Poets
Anahit Arustamyan * Yvette D. Murrell * Regina A. Walker

Pearl

The Poetry Posse 2015
Jamie Bond * Gail Weston Shazor * Albert 'Infinite' Carrasco
Siddartha Beth Pierce * Janet P. Caldwell * Tony Henninger
Joe DaVerbal Minddancer * Neetu Wali * Shareef Abdur – Rasheed
Kimberly Burnham * Ann White * Keith Alan Hamilton
Katherine Wyatt * Fahredin Shehu * Hülya N. Yılmaz
Teresa E. Gallion * Jackie Allen * William S. Peters, Sr.

The Year of the Poet II
July 2015

The Featured Poets for July 2015
Abhik Shome * Christina Neal * Robert Neal

Rubies

The Poetry Posse 2015
Jamie Bond * Gail Weston Shazor * Albert 'Infinite' Carrasco
Siddartha Beth Pierce * Janet P. Caldwell * Tony Henninger
Joe DaVerbal Minddancer * Neetu Wali * Shareef Abdur – Rasheed
Kimberly Burnham * Ann White * Keith Alan Hamilton
Katherine Wyatt * Fahredin Shehu * Hülya N. Yılmaz
Teresa E. Gallion * Jackie Allen * William S. Peters, Sr.

The Year of the Poet II
August 2015

Peridot

Featured Poets
Gayle Howell
Ann Chalasz
Christopher Schultz

The Poetry Posse 2015
Jamie Bond * Gail Weston Shazor * Albert 'Infinite' Carrasco
Siddartha Beth Pierce * Janet P. Caldwell * Tony Henninger
Joe DaVerbal Minddancer * Neetu Wali * Shareef Abdur – Rasheed
Kimberly Burnham * Ann White * Keith Alan Hamilton
Katherine Wyatt * Fahredin Shehu * Hülya N. Yılmaz
Teresa E. Gallion * Jackie Allen * William S. Peters, Sr.

Now Available
www.innerchildpress.com/the-year-of-the-poet

The Year of the Poet II
September 2015

Featured Poets
Alfreda Ghee * Lonnsion Wonks Dudley * Demetrius Thisatis

Sapphires

The Poetry Posse 2015
Jamie Bond * Gail Weston Shazor * Albert 'Infinite' Carrasco
Siddartha Beth Pierce * Janet P. Caldwell * Tony Henninger
Joe DaVerbal Minddancer * Neetu Wali * Shareef Abdur – Rasheed
Kimberly Burnham * Ann White * Keith Alan Hamilton
Katherine Wyatt * Fahredin Shehu * Hülya N. Yılmaz
Teresa E. Gallion * Jackie Allen * William S. Peters, Sr.

The Year of the Poet II
October 2015

Featured Poets
Maaia Bulalu * Laura J. Wolfe * William Washington

Opal

The Poetry Posse 2015
Jamie Bond * Gail Weston Shazor * Albert 'Infinite' Carrasco
Siddartha Beth Pierce * Janet P. Caldwell * Tony Henninger
Joe DaVerbal Minddancer * Neetu Wali * Shareef Abdur – Rasheed
Kimberly Burnham * Ann White * Keith Alan Hamilton
Katherine Wyatt * Fahredin Shehu * Hülya N. Yılmaz
Teresa E. Gallion * Jackie Allen * William S. Peters, Sr.

The Year of the Poet II
November 2015

Featured Poets
Alan W. Jankowski
Bisnay Mohanty
James Moore

Topaz

The Poetry Posse 2015
Jamie Bond * Gail Weston Shazor * Albert 'Infinite' Carrasco
Siddartha Beth Pierce * Janet P. Caldwell * Tony Henninger
Joe DaVerbal Minddancer * Neetu Wali * Shareef Abdur – Rasheed
Kimberly Burnham * Ann White * Keith Alan Hamilton
Katherine Wyatt * Fahredin Shehu * Hülya N. Yılmaz
Teresa E. Gallion * Jackie Allen * William S. Peters, Sr.

The Year of the Poet II
December 2015

Featured Poets
Kerione Bryan * Michelle Joan Barulich * Neville Hiatt

Turquoise

The Poetry Posse 2015
Jamie Bond * Gail Weston Shazor * Albert 'Infinite' Carrasco
Siddartha Beth Pierce * Janet P. Caldwell * Tony Henninger
Joe DaVerbal Minddancer * Neetu Wali * Shareef Abdur – Rasheed
Kimberly Burnham * Ann White * Keith Alan Hamilton
Katherine Wyatt * Fahredin Shehu * Hülya N. Yılmaz
Teresa E. Gallion * Jackie Allen * William S. Peters, Sr.

Now Available

www.innerchildpress.com/the-year-of-the-poet

The Year of the Poet III
January 2016

Featured Poets
Lana Joseph * Atom Cyrus Rush * Christena Williams

Dark-eyed Junco

The Poetry Posse 2016
Gail Weston Shazor * Anna Jakubczak Vel Ratty Adalan * Ann J. White
Fahredin Shehu * Hrishikesh Padhye * Janet P. Caldwell
Joe DaVerbal Minddancer * Shareef Abdur - Rasheed
Albert Carrasco * Kimberly Burnham * Keith Alan Hamilton
Hülya N. Yılmaz * Demetrios Trifiatis * Alan W. Jankowski
Teresa E. Gallion * Jackie Davis Allen * William S. Peters, Sr.

The Year of the Poet III
February 2016

Featured Poets
Anthony Arnold
Anna Chalasz
Andre Balo-borne

Puffin

The Poetry Posse 2016
Gail Weston Shazor * Joe DaVerbal Minddancer * Alfreda Ghee
Fahredin Shehu * Hrishikesh Padhye * Janet P. Caldwell
Anna Jakubczak Vel Ratty Adalan * Shareef Abdur - Rasheed
Albert Carrasco * Kimberly Burnham * Ann J. White
Hülya N. Yılmaz * Demetrios Trifiatis * Alan W. Jankowski
Teresa E. Gallion * Jackie Davis Allen * William S. Peters, Sr.

The Year of the Poet III
March 2016
Featured Poets
Jeton Kelmendi   Nizar Sartawi   Sami Muhanna

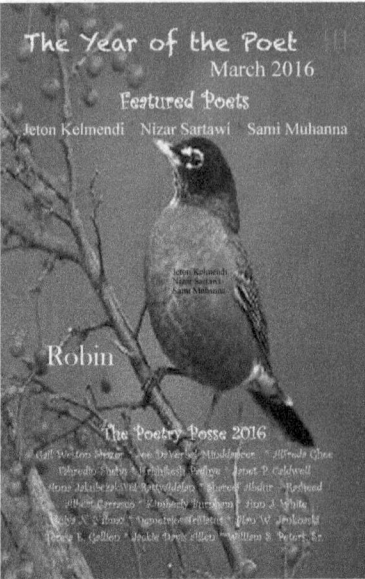

Robin

The Poetry Posse 2016
Gail Weston Shazor * Joe DaVerbal Minddancer * Alfreda Ghee
Fahredin Shehu * Hrishikesh Padhye * Janet P. Caldwell
Anna Jakubczak Vel Ratty Adalan * Shareef Abdur - Rasheed
Albert Carrasco * Kimberly Burnham * Ann J. White
Hülya N. Yılmaz * Demetrios Trifiatis * Alan W. Jankowski
Teresa E. Gallion * Jackie Davis Allen * William S. Peters, Sr.

The Year of the Poet III

Featured Poets
Ali Abdolrezaei

Anna Chalasz

Agim Vinca

Ceri Naz

Black Capped Chickadee

The Poetry Posse 2016
Gail Weston Shazor * Joe DaVerbal Minddancer * Alfreda Ghee
Fahredin Shehu * Hrishikesh Padhye * Janet P. Caldwell
Anna Jakubczak Vel Ratty Adalan * Shareef Abdur - Rasheed
Albert Carrasco * Kimberly Burnham * Ann J. White
Hülya N. Yılmaz * Demetrios Trifiatis * Alan W. Jankowski
Teresa E. Gallion * Jackie Davis Allen * William S. Peters, Sr.

celebrating international poetry month

Now Available
www.innerchildpress.com/the-year-of-the-poet

The Year of the Poet
May 2016

Bob Strum
Barbara Allan
D.L. Davis

Oriole

The Poetry Posse 2016

The Year of the Poet III
June 2016

Featured Poets

Qibrije Demhi Mangu
Naime Beqiraj
Faleeha Hassan
Bedri Zyberaj

Black Necked Stilt

The Poetry Posse 2016

The Year of the Poet III
July 2016

Featured Poets

Iram Fatima 'Ashi'
Langley Shazor
Jody Doty
Emilia T. Davis

Indigo Bunting

The Poetry Posse 2016

The Year of the Poet III
August 2016

Featured Poets

Anita Dash
Irena Jovanovic
Malgorzata Gouluda

Painted Bunting

The Poetry Posse 2016

Now Available

www.innerchildpress.com/the-year-of-the-poet

The Year of the Poet III
September 2016

Featured Poets

Simone Weber
Abhijit Sen
Eunice Barbara C. Novio

Long Billed Curle

The Poetry Posse 2016

The Year of the Poet III
October 2016

Featured Poets

Lana Joseph
Krishnamurthy R
James Moore

Barn Owl

The Poetry Posse 2016

The Year of the Poet III
November 2016

Featured Poets

Rosemary Burns
Robin Ouzman Hislop
Lonneice Weeks-Badley

Northern Cardinal

The Poetry Posse 2016

The Year of the Poet III
December 2016

Featured Poets

Samih Masoud
Mountassir Aziz Bien
Abdulkadir Musa

Rough Legged Hawk

The Poetry Posse 2016

Now Available

www.innerchildpress.com/the-year-of-the-poet

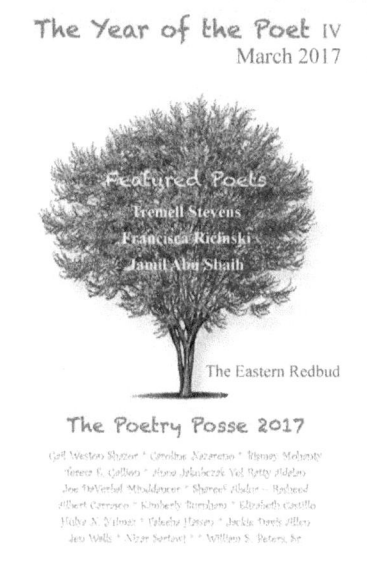

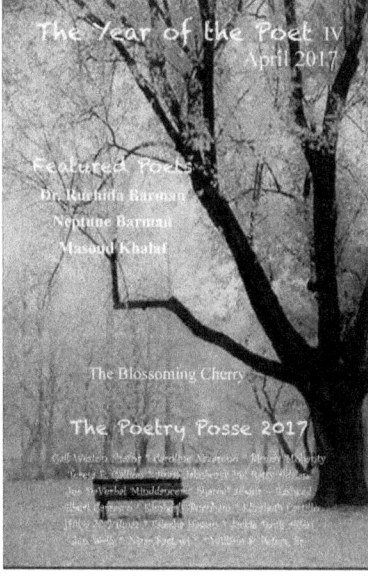

The Year of the Poet IV
January 2017

Featured Poets
Jon Winell
Natalie Shields
Irani Fatima Asht

Quaking Aspen

The Poetry Posse 2017

The Year of the Poet IV
February 2017

Featured Poets
Lin Ross
Soukaina Fathi
Anwer Ghani

Witch Hazel

The Poetry Posse 2017

The Year of the Poet IV
March 2017

Featured Poets
Tremell Stevens
Francisca Ricinski
Jamil Abu Shaih

The Eastern Redbud

The Poetry Posse 2017

The Year of the Poet IV
April 2017

Featured Poets
Dr. Rachida Barman
Neptune Barman
Masood Khalaf

The Blossoming Cherry

The Poetry Posse 2017

Now Available
www.innerchildpress.com/the-year-of-the-poet

The Year of the Poet IV
May 2017

The Flowering Dogwood Tree

Featured Poets
Kallisa Powell
Alicja Maria Kuberska
Fethi Sassi

The Poetry Posse 2017

Gail Weston Shazor * Caroline Nazareno * Jhimmy Mohanty
Teresa E. Gallion * Anna Jakubczak Val Retty Adelan
Joe DaVerbal Minddancer * Shareef Abdur – Rasheed
Albert Carrasco * Kimberly Burnham * Elizabeth Castillo
Hülya N. Yılmaz * Eolosha Hogans * Jackie Davis Allen
Jen Walls * Nizar Sartawi * * William S. Peters, Sr.

The Year of the Poet IV
June 2017

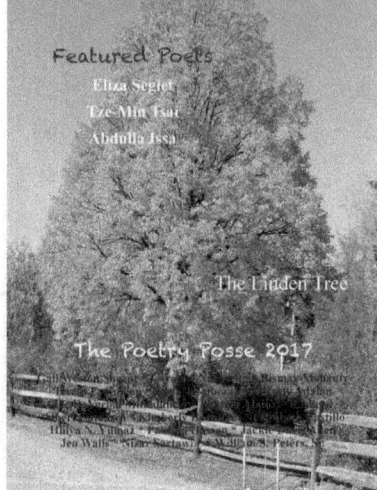

Featured Poets
Eliza Segiet
Tze-Min Tsai
Abdulla Issa

The Linden Tree

The Poetry Posse 2017

Hülya N. Yılmaz
Jen Walls * Nizar Sartawi * William S. Peters, Sr.

The Year of the Poet IV
July 2017

Featured Poets
Anca Mihaela Bruma
Ibaa Ismail
Zvonko Taneski

The Oak Moon

The Poetry Posse 2017

The Year of the Poet IV
August 2017

Featured Poets
Jonathan Aquino
Kitty Hsu
Langley Shazor

The Hazelnut Tree

The Poetry Posse 2017

Gail Weston Shazor * Caroline Nazareno *
Teresa E. Gallion * Anna Jakubczak Val Retty Adelan
Joe DaVerbal Minddancer * Shareef Abdur – Rasheed
Albert Carrasco * Kimberly Burnham * Elizabeth Castillo
Hülya N. Yılmaz * Eolosha Hogans * Jackie Davis Allen
Jen Walls * Nizar Sartawi * * William S. Peters, Sr.

Now Available
www.innerchildpress.com/the-year-of-the-poet

222

The Year of the Poet IV
September 2017

Featured Poets

Martina Reisz Newberry
Aimeer Nassir
Christine Fulco Neal
Robert Neal

The Elm Tree

The Poetry Posse 2017

Gail Weston Shazor * Caroline Nazareno * Bismay Mohanty
Teresa E. Gallion * Anna Jakubczak Vel Ratty Adalan
Joe DaVerbal Minddancer * Shareef Abdur – Rasheed
Albert Carrasco * Kimberly Burnham * Elizabeth Castillo
Hülya N. Yılmaz * Faleeha Hassan * Jackie Davis Allen
Jen Walls * Nizar Sartawi * * William S. Peters, Sr.

The Year of the Poet IV
October 2017

Featured Poets

Ahmed Abu Saleem
Nedal Al-Qaeim
3adeddin Shahin

The Black Walnut Tree

The Poetry Posse 2017

Gail Weston Shazor * Caroline Nazareno * Bismay Mohanty
Teresa E. Gallion * Anna Jakubczak Vel Ratty Adalan
Joe DaVerbal Minddancer * Shareef Abdur – Rasheed
Albert Carrasco * Kimberly Burnham * Elizabeth Castillo
Hülya N. Yılmaz * Faleeha Hassan * Jackie Davis Allen
Jen Walls * Nizar Sartawi * William S. Peters, Sr.

The Year of the Poet IV
November 2017

Featured Poets

Kay Peters
Alfreda D. Ghee
Gabriella Garofalo
Rosemary Cappello

The Tree of Life

The Poetry Posse 2017

Gail Weston Shazor * Caroline Nazareno * Bismay Mohanty
Teresa E. Gallion * Anna Jakubczak Vel Ratty Adalan
Joe DaVerbal Minddancer * Shareef Abdur – Rasheed
Albert Carrasco * Kimberly Burnham * Elizabeth Castillo
Hülya N. Yılmaz * Faleeha Hassan * Jackie Davis Allen
Jen Walls * Nizar Sartawi * William S. Peters, Sr.

The Year of the Poet IV
December 2017

Featured Poets

Justice Clarke
Mariel M. Pabroa
Kiley Brown

The Fig Tree

The Poetry Posse 2017

Gail Weston Shazor * Caroline Nazareno * Bismay Mohanty
Teresa E. Gallion * Anna Jakubczak Vel Ratty Adalan
Joe DaVerbal Minddancer * Shareef Abdur – Rasheed
Albert Carrasco * Kimberly Burnham * Elizabeth Castillo
Hülya N. Yılmaz * Faleeha Hassan * Jackie Davis Allen
Jen Walls * Nizar Sartawi * William S. Peters, Sr.

Now Available

www.innerchildpress.com/the-year-of-the-poet

The Year of the Poet V
January 2018
Featured Poets

Iyad Shamasnah

Yasmeen Hamzeh

Ali Abdolrezaei

Aksum

The Poetry Posse 2018

Gail Weston Shazor * Caroline Nazareno * Tezmin Ition Tsai
Hülya N. Yılmaz * Faleeha Hassan * Jackie Davis Allen
Teresa E. Gallion * Anna Jakubczak Vel Ratty Adalan
Alicja Maria Kuberska * Shareef Abdur – Rasheed
Kimberly Burnham * Elizabeth Castillo
Nizar Sartawi * William S. Peters, Sr.

The Year of the Poet V
February 2018

Sabean

Featured Poets

Muhammad Azram

Anna Szawracka

Abhilipsa Kuanar

Aamka Aery

The Poetry Posse 2018

Gail Weston Shazor * Caroline Nazareno * Tezmin Ition Tsai
Hülya N. Yılmaz * Faleeha Hassan * Jackie Davis Allen
Teresa E. Gallion * Anna Jakubczak Vel Ratty Adalan
Alicja Maria Kuberska * Shareef Abdur – Rasheed
Kimberly Burnham * Elizabeth Castillo
Nizar Sartawi * William S. Peters, Sr.

The Year of the Poet V
March 2018

Featured Poets

Iram Fatima 'Ashi'
Cassandra Swan
Jaleel Khazaal
Shazia Zaman

Mexico   Cuba

Caribbean
&
Middle America

The Poetry Posse 2018

Gail Weston Shazor * Nizar Sartawi * Hülya N. Yılmaz
Jackie Davis Allen * Caroline 'Ceri' Nazareno
Alicja Maria Kuberska * Teresa E. Gallion
Faleeha Hassan * Shareef Abdur – Rasheed
Kimberly Burnham * Elizabeth Castillo
Tezmin Ition Tsai * William S. Peters, Sr.

The Year of the Poet V
April 2018

Featured Poets

The Nez Perce

The Poetry Posse 2018

Now Available
www.innerchildpress.com/the-year-of-the-poet

The Year of the Poet V
May 2018

Featured Poets

Teddy Crescent; S. Lawal;
Sylwia K. Malinowska;
Lindita Afrimi;
Olëta Prodani

The Sumerians

The Poetry Posse 2018

Gail Weston Shazor * Nizar Sartawi * Hülya N. Yılmaz
Jackie Davis Allen * Caroline 'Ceri' Nazareno
Alicja Maria Kuberska * Teresa E. Gallion
Kimberly Burnham * Shareef Abdur ~ Rasheed
Faleeha Hassan * Elizabeth Castillo * Swapna Behera
Tezmin Ition Tsai * William S. Peters, Sr.

The Year of the Poet V
June 2018

Featured Poets

Bilall Maliqi * Daim Miftari * Gojko Božović * Sofija Živković

The Paleo Indians

The Poetry Posse 2018

Gail Weston Shazor * Nizar Sartawi * Hülya N. Yılmaz
Jackie Davis Allen * Caroline 'Ceri' Nazareno
Alicja Maria Kuberska * Teresa E. Gallion
Kimberly Burnham * Shareef Abdur ~ Rasheed
Faleeha Hassan * Elizabeth Castillo * Swapna Behera
Tezmin Ition Tsai * William S. Peters, Sr.

The Year of the Poet V
July 2018

Featured Poets

Padraig Treanor-Paddy
Mohammad Ikbal Harb
Eliza Segiet
Tom Higgins

Oceania

The Poetry Posse 2018

Gail Weston Shazor * Nizar Sartawi * Hülya N. Yılmaz
Jackie Davis Allen * Caroline 'Ceri' Nazareno
Alicja Maria Kuberska * Teresa E. Gallion
Kimberly Burnham * Shareef Abdur ~ Rasheed
Faleeha Hassan * Elizabeth Castillo * Swapna Behera
Tezmin Ition Tsai * William S. Peters, Sr.

The Year of the Poet V
August 2018

Featured Poets

Hussein Habasch * Mircea Dan Duta * Naida Mujkić * Swagat Das

The Lapita

The Poetry Posse 2018

Gail Weston Shazor * Nizar Sartawi * Hülya N. Yılmaz
Jackie Davis Allen * Caroline 'Ceri' Nazareno
Alicja Maria Kuberska * Teresa E. Gallion
Kimberly Burnham * Shareef Abdur ~ Rasheed
Ashok K. Bhargava* Elizabeth Castillo * Swapna Behaera
Tezmin Ition Tsai * William S. Peters, Sr.

Now Available

www.innerchildpress.com/the-year-of-the-poet

The Year of the Poet V
September 2018

The Aztecs & Incas

Featured Poets
Kolade Olanrewaju Freedom
Eliza Segiet
Mazher Hussain Abdul Ghani
Lily Swarn

The Poetry Posse 2018

Gail Weston Shazor * Nizar Sartawi * Hülya N. Yılmaz
Jackie Davis Allen * Caroline 'Ceri' Nazareno
Alicja Maria Kuberska * Teresa E. Gallion
Kimberly Burnham * Shareef Abdur – Rasheed
Ashok K. Bhargava * Elizabeth Castillo * Swapna Behera
Tezmin Ition Tsai * William S. Peters, Sr.

The Year of the Poet V
October 2018

Featured Poets
Alicia Minjarez * Lonneice Weeks-Badley
Lopamudra Mishra * Abdelwahed Souayah

Bengali

The Poetry Posse 2018

Gail Weston Shazor * Nizar Sartawi * Hülya N. Yılmaz
Jackie Davis Allen * Caroline 'Ceri' Nazareno
Alicja Maria Kuberska * Teresa E. Gallion
Kimberly Burnham * Shareef Abdur – Rasheed
Ashok K. Bhargava * Elizabeth Castillo * Swapna Behera
Tezmin Ition Tsai * William S. Peters, Sr.

The Year of the Poet V
November 2018

Featured Poets
Michelle Joan Barulich * Monsif Beroual
Krystyna Konecka * Nassira Nezzar

The Poetry Posse 2018

Gail Weston Shazor * Nizar Sartawi * Hülya N. Yılmaz
Jackie Davis Allen * Caroline 'Ceri' Nazareno
Alicja Maria Kuberska * Teresa E. Gallion
Kimberly Burnham * Shareef Abdur – Rasheed
Ashok K. Bhargava * Elizabeth Castillo * Swapna Behera
Tezmin Ition Tsai * William S. Peters, Sr.

The Year of the Poet V
December 2018

Featured Poets
Rose Terranova Cirigliano
Joanna Kalinowska
Sokolović Emir
Dr. T. Ashok Chakravarthy

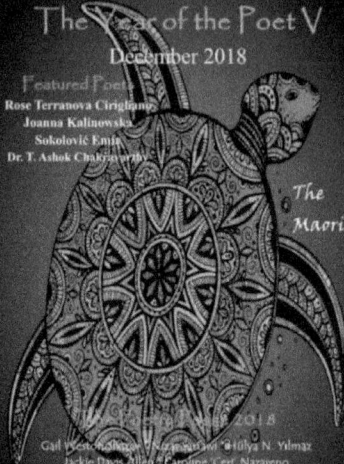

The Maori

The Poetry Posse 2018

Gail Weston Shazor * Nizar Sartawi * Hülya N. Yılmaz
Jackie Davis Allen * Caroline 'Ceri' Nazareno
Alicja Maria Kuberska * Teresa E. Gallion
Kimberly Burnham * Shareef Abdur – Rasheed
Ashok K. Bhargava * Elizabeth Castillo * Swapna Behera
Tezmin Ition Tsai * William S. Peters, Sr.

Now Available

www.innerchildpress.com/the-year-of-the-poet

The Year of the Poet V I
January 2019

Indigenous North Americans

Featured Poets

Honda Elfehtali
Anthony Briscoe
Iram Fatima 'Ashi'
Dr. K. K. Mathew

Dream Catcher

The Poetry Posse 2019

Gail Weston Shazor * Joe Paire * Hülya N. Yilmaz
Jackie Davis Allen * Caroline Cori Nazareno
Alicja Maria Kubenska * Teresa E. Gallion
Kimberly Burnham * Shareef Abdur – Rasheed
Ashok K. Bhargava * Elizabeth Castillo * Swapna Behera
Tezmin Ition Tsai * William S. Peters, Sr.

The Year of the Poet VI
February 2019

Featured Poets

Marek Lukaszewicz * Bharati Nayak
Aida G. Roque * Jean-Jacques Fournier

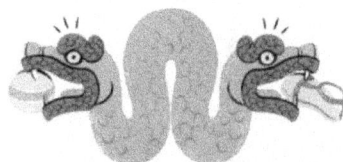

Meso-America

The Poetry Posse 2019

Gail Weston Shazor * Albert Carasco * Hülya N. Yilmaz
Jackie Davis Allen * Caroline Nazareno * Eliza Segiet
Alicja Maria Kubenska * Teresa E. Gallion * Joe Paire
Kimberly Burnham * Shareef Abdur – Rasheed
Ashok K. Bhargava * Elizabeth Castillo * Swapna Behera
Tezmin Ition Tsai * William S. Peters, Sr.

The Year of the Poet VI
March 2019

Featured Poets

Enesa Mahmić * Sylwia K. Malinowska
Shurouk Hammoud * Anwer Ghani

The Caribbean

The Poetry Posse 2019

Gail Weston Shazor * Albert Carasco * Hülya N. Yilmaz
Jackie Davis Allen * Caroline Nazareno * Eliza Segiet
Alicja Maria Kubenska * Teresa E. Gallion * Joe Paire
Kimberly Burnham * Shareef Abdur – Rasheed
Ashok K. Bhargava * Elizabeth Castillo * Swapna Behera
Tezmin Ition Tsai * William S. Peters, Sr.

The Year of the Poet VI
April 2019

Featured Poets

DL Davis * Michelle Joan Barulich
Lulëzim Haziri * Faleeha Hassan

Central & West Africa

The Poetry Posse 2019

Gail Weston Shazor * Albert Carasco * Hülya N. Yilmaz
Jackie Davis Allen * Caroline Nazareno * Eliza Segiet
Alicja Maria Kubenska * Teresa E. Gallion * Joe Paire
Kimberly Burnham * Shareef Abdur – Rasheed
Ashok K. Bhargava * Elizabeth Castillo * Swapna Behera
Tezmin Ition Tsai * William S. Peters, Sr.

Now Available

www.innerchildpress.com/the-year-of-the-poet

Now Available

www.innerchildpress.com/the-year-of-the-poet

The Year of the Poet VI
September 2019
Featured Poets
Elena Liliana Popescu * Orbindu Ganga
Iram Fatima 'Ashi' * Joseph S. Spence, Sr.

The Caucasus
The Poetry Posse 2019

Gail Weston Shazor * Albert Carrasco * Hülya N. Yılmaz
Jackie Davis Allen * Caroline Nazareno * Eliza Segiet
Alicja Maria Kuberska * Teresa E. Gallion * Joe Paire
Kimberly Burnham * Shareef Abdur – Rasheed
Ashok K. Bhargava * Elizabeth Castillo * Swapna Behera
Tzemin Ition Tsai * William S. Peters, Sr.

The Year of the Poet VI
October 2019
Featured Poets
Tigali Olivia Osobu * Denisa Kondić
Pankhuri Sinha * Chrisiena AV Williams

The Nile Valley
The Poetry Posse 2019

Gail Weston Shazor * Albert Carrasco * Hülya N. Yılmaz
Jackie Davis Allen * Caroline Nazareno * Eliza Segiet
Alicja Maria Kuberska * Teresa E. Gallion * Joe Paire
Kimberly Burnham * Shareef Abdur – Rasheed
Ashok K. Bhargava * Elizabeth Castillo * Swapna Behera
Tzemin Ition Tsai * William S. Peters, Sr.

The Year of the Poet VI
November 2019
Featured Poets
Rozalia Aleksandrova * Orbindu Ganga
Smruti Ranjan Mohanty * Sofia Skleida

Northern Asia
The Poetry Posse 2019

Gail Weston Shazor * Albert Carrasco * Hülya N. Yılmaz
Jackie Davis Allen * Caroline Nazareno * Eliza Segiet
Alicja Maria Kuberska * Teresa E. Gallion * Joe Paire
Kimberly Burnham * Shareef Abdur – Rasheed
Ashok K. Bhargava * Elizabeth Castillo * Swapna Behera
Tzemin Ition Tsai * William S. Peters, Sr.

The Year of the Poet VI
December 2019
Featured Poets
Rahim Karim (Karimov) * Sonali Pant
Bhaumik Nayak * Kapardeli Eftichia

Oceania
The Poetry Posse 2019

Gail Weston Shazor * Albert Carrasco * Hülya N. Yılmaz
Jackie Davis Allen * Caroline Nazareno * Eliza Segiet
Alicja Maria Kuberska * Teresa E. Gallion * Joe Paire
Kimberly Burnham * Shareef Abdur – Rasheed
Ashok K. Bhargava * Elizabeth Castillo * Swapna Behera
Tzemin Ition Tsai * William S. Peters, Sr.

Now Available
www.innerchildpress.com/the-year-of-the-poet

The Year of the Poet VII

January 2020

Featured Poets

B S Tyagi * Ashok Chakravarthy Tholana
Andy Scott * Anwer Ghani

1901 Jean Henry Dunant and Frédéric Passy

The Year of Peace
Celebrating past Nobel Peace Prize Recipients

The Poetry Posse 2020

Gail Weston Shazor * Albert Carasico * Hülya N. Yılmaz
Jackie Davis Allen * Caroline Nazareno * Eliza Segiet
Alicja Maria Kuberska * Teresa E. Gallion * Joe Paire
Kimberly Burnham * Shareef Abdur – Rasheed
Ashok K. Bhargava * Elizabeth Castillo * Swapna Behera
Tezmin Ition Tsai * William S. Peters, Sr.

The Year of the Poet VII

February 2020

Featured Poets

Jennifer Ades * Martina Reisz Newberry
Ibrahim Honjo * Claudia Piccinno

Henri La Fontaine ~ 1913

The Year of Peace
Celebrating past Nobel Peace Prize Recipients

The Poetry Posse 2020

Gail Weston Shazor * Albert Carasico * Hülya N. Yılmaz
Jackie Davis Allen * Caroline Nazareno * Eliza Segiet
Alicja Maria Kuberska * Teresa E. Gallion * Joe Paire
Kimberly Burnham * Shareef Abdur – Rasheed
Ashok K. Bhargava * Elizabeth Castillo * Swapna Behera
Tezmin Ition Tsai * William S. Peters, Sr.

The Year of the Poet VII

March 2020

Featured Poets

Aziz Mountassir * Krishna Paraisa
Hannie Rouweler * Rozalia Aleksandrova

Aristide Briand ~ 1926 ~ Gustav Stresemann

The Year of Peace
Celebrating past Nobel Peace Prize Recipients

The Poetry Posse 2020

Gail Weston Shazor * Albert Carasico * Hülya N. Yılmaz
Jackie Davis Allen * Caroline Nazareno * Eliza Segiet
Alicja Maria Kuberska * Teresa E. Gallion * Joe Paire
Kimberly Burnham * Shareef Abdur – Rasheed
Ashok K. Bhargava * Elizabeth Castillo * Swapna Behera
Tezmin Ition Tsai * William S. Peters, Sr.

The Year of the Poet VII

April 2020

Featured Poets

Rohini Behera * Mircea Dan Duta
Monalisa Dash Dwibedy * NilavroNill Shoovro

Carlos Saavedra Lamas ~ 1936

The Year of Peace
Celebrating past Nobel Peace Prize Recipients

The Poetry Posse 2020

Gail Weston Shazor * Albert Carasico * Hülya N. Yılmaz
Jackie Davis Allen * Caroline Nazareno * Eliza Segiet
Alicja Maria Kuberska * Teresa E. Gallion * Joe Paire
Kimberly Burnham * Shareef Abdur – Rasheed
Ashok K. Bhargava * Elizabeth Castillo * Swapna Behera
Tezmin Ition Tsai * William S. Peters, Sr.

Now Available

www.innerchildpress.com/the-year-of-the-poet

The Year of the Poet VII
May 2020

Featured Poets
Alok Kumar Ray * Eden S. Trinidad
Franci Barnada * Izabela Zubko

Ralph Bunche ~ 1950

The Year of Peace
Celebrating past Nobel Peace Prize Recipients

The Poetry Posse 2020
Gail Weston Shazor * Albert Carasco * Hülya N. Yılmaz
Jackie Davis Allen * Caroline Nazareno * Eliza Segiet
Alicja Maria Kuberska * Teresa E. Gallion * Joe Paire
Kimberly Burnham * Shareef Abdur – Rasheed
Ashok K. Bhargava * Elizabeth Castillo * Swapna Behera
Tezmin Ition Tsai * William S. Peters, Sr.

The Year of the Poet VII
June 2020

Featured Poets
Filicia Kapardeli * Melin Cengiz
Hussein Habasch * Kosh K Mathew

Albert John Lutuli ~ 1960

The Year of Peace
Celebrating past Nobel Peace Prize Recipients

The Poetry Posse 2020
Gail Weston Shazor * Albert Carasco * Hülya N. Yılmaz
Jackie Davis Allen * Caroline Nazareno * Eliza Segiet
Alicja Maria Kuberska * Teresa E. Gallion * Joe Paire
Kimberly Burnham * Shareef Abdur – Rasheed
Ashok K. Bhargava * Elizabeth Castillo * Swapna Behera
Tezmin Ition Tsai * William S. Peters, Sr.

The Year of the Poet VII
July 2020

Featured Poets
Mykola Martyniuk * Orbindu Ganga
Roula Pollard * Karn Praktisha

Norman Ernest Borlaug ~ 1970

The Year of Peace
Celebrating past Nobel Peace Prize Recipients

The Poetry Posse 2020
Gail Weston Shazor * Albert Carasco * Hülya N. Yılmaz
Jackie Davis Allen * Caroline Nazareno * Eliza Segiet
Alicja Maria Kuberska * Teresa E. Gallion * Joe Paire
Kimberly Burnham * Shareef Abdur – Rasheed
Ashok K. Bhargava * Elizabeth Castillo * Swapna Behera
Tezmin Ition Tsai * William S. Peters, Sr.

The Year of the Poet VII
August 2020

Featured Poets
Dr Pragya Suman * Chinh Nguyen
Srinivas Vasudev * Ugwu Leonard Ifeanyi, Jr.

Adolfo Pérez Esquivel ~ 1980

The Year of Peace
Celebrating past Nobel Peace Prize Recipients

The Poetry Posse 2020
Gail Weston Shazor * Albert Carasco * Hülya N. Yılmaz
Jackie Davis Allen * Caroline Nazareno * Eliza Segiet
Alicja Maria Kuberska * Teresa E. Gallion * Joe Paire
Kimberly Burnham * Shareef Abdur – Rasheed
Ashok K. Bhargava * Elizabeth Castillo * Swapna Behera
Tezmin Ition Tsai * William S. Peters, Sr.

Now Available

www.innerchildpress.com/the-year-of-the-poet

The Year of the Poet VII

September 2020

Featured Poets

Raed Anis Al-Jishi • Srdkjrtovic Snetana
Dr. Brojesh Kumar Gupta • Umid Najjari

Mikhail Sergeyevich Gorbachev ~ 1990

The Year of Peace
Celebrating past Nobel Peace Prize Recipients

The Poetry Posse 2020

Gail Weston Shazor • Albert Carasco • Hülya N. Yılmaz
Jackie Davis Allen • Caroline Nazareno • Eliza Segiet
Alicja Maria Kubersla • Teresa E. Gallion • Joe Paire
Kimberly Burnham • Shareef Abdur – Rasheed
Ashok K. Bhargava • Elizabeth Castillo • Swapna Behera
Tezmin Ition Tsai • William S. Peters, Sr.

The Year of the Poet VII

October 2020

Featured Poets

Mutawaf A. Shaheed • Galina Italyanskaya
Nadeem Fraz • Avril Tanya Meallem

Kim Dae-jung ~ 2000

The Year of Peace
Celebrating past Nobel Peace Prize Recipients

The Poetry Posse 2020

Gail Weston Shazor • Albert Carasco • Hülya N. Yılmaz
Jackie Davis Allen • Caroline Nazareno • Eliza Segiet
Alicja Maria Kubersla • Teresa E. Gallion • Joe Paire
Kimberly Burnham • Shareef Abdur – Rasheed
Ashok K. Bhargava • Elizabeth Castillo • Swapna Behera
Tezmin Ition Tsai • William S. Peters, Sr.

The Year of the Poet VII

November 2020

Featured Poets

Elisa Mascia • Sue Lindenberg McClelland
Hatif Janabi • Ivan Gacina

Liu Xiaobo ~ 2010

The Year of Peace
Celebrating past Nobel Peace Prize Recipients

The Poetry Posse 2020

Gail Weston Shazor • Albert Carasco • Hülya N. Yılmaz
Jackie Davis Allen • Caroline Nazareno • Eliza Segiet
Alicja Maria Kubersla • Teresa E. Gallion • Joe Paire
Kimberly Burnham • Shareef Abdur – Rasheed
Ashok K. Bhargava • Elizabeth Castillo • Swapna Behera
Tezmin Ition Tsai • William S. Peters, Sr.

The Year of the Poet VII

December 2020

Featured Poets

Ratan Ghosh • Ibtisam Ibrahim Al-Asady
Brindha Vinodh • Selma Kopic

Abiy Ahmed Ali ~ 2019

The Year of Peace
Celebrating past Nobel Peace Prize Recipients

The Poetry Posse 2020

Gail Weston Shazor • Albert Carasco • Hülya N. Yılmaz
Jackie Davis Allen • Caroline Nazareno • Eliza Segiet
Alicja Maria Kubersla • Teresa E. Gallion • Joe Paire
Kimberly Burnham • Shareef Abdur – Rasheed
Ashok K. Bhargava • Elizabeth Castillo • Swapna Behera
Tezmin Ition Tsai • William S. Peters, Sr.

Now Available

www.innerchildpress.com/the-year-of-the-poet

The Year of the Poet VIII
January 2021
Featured Global Poets
Andrew Scott * Debaprasanna Biswas
Bhakti Kalani * Changming Yuan

Banksy's The Girl with the Pierced Eardrum

Poetry ... Ekphrasticly Speaking
The Poetry Posse 2020
Gail Weston Shazor * Albert Carasco * Hülya N. Yılmaz
Jackie Davis Allen * Caroline Nazareno * Eliza Segiet
Alicja Maria Kuberska * Teresa E. Gallion * Joe Paire
Kimberly Burnham * Shareef Abdur – Rasheed
Ashok K. Bhargava * Elizabeth Castillo * Swapna Behera
Tezmin Ition Tsai * William S. Peters, Sr.

The Year of the Poet VIII
February 2021
Featured Global Poets
T. Ramesh Babu * Ruchida Barman
Neptune Barman * Faleeha Hassan

Emory Douglas : 1968 Olympics mural

Poetry ... Ekphrasticly Speaking
The Poetry Posse 2021
Gail Weston Shazor * Albert Carasco * Hülya N. Yılmaz
Jackie Davis Allen * Caroline Nazareno * Eliza Segiet
Alicja Maria Kuberska * Teresa E. Gallion * Joe Paire
Kimberly Burnham * Shareef Abdur – Rasheed
Ashok K. Bhargava * Elizabeth Castillo * Swapna Behera
Tezmin Ition Tsai * William S. Peters, Sr.

The Year of the Poet VIII
March 2021
Featured Global Poets
Claudia Piccinno * Mohammed Jabr
Luzviminda Rivera * Nigar Arif

Tatyana Fazlalizadeh

Poetry ... Ekphrasticly Speaking
The Poetry Posse 2021
Gail Weston Shazor * Albert Carasco * Hülya N. Yılmaz
Jackie Davis Allen * Caroline Nazareno * Eliza Segiet
Alicja Maria Kuberska * Teresa E. Gallion * Joe Paire
Kimberly Burnham * Shareef Abdur – Rasheed
Ashok K. Bhargava * Elizabeth Castillo * Swapna Behera
Tezmin Ition Tsai * William S. Peters, Sr.

The Year of the Poet VIII
April 2021
Featured Global Poets
Katarzyna Brus- Sawczuk * Anwesha Paul
Rozalia Aleksandrova * Shahid Abbas

Pablo O'Higgins

Poetry ... Ekphrasticly Speaking
The Poetry Posse 2021
Gail Weston Shazor * Albert Carasco * Hülya N. Yılmaz
Jackie Davis Allen * Caroline Nazareno * Eliza Segiet
Alicja Maria Kuberska * Teresa E. Gallion * Joe Paire
Kimberly Burnham * Shareef Abdur – Rasheed
Ashok K. Bhargava * Elizabeth Castillo * Swapna Behera
Tezmin Ition Tsai * William S. Peters, Sr.

Now Available
www.innerchildpress.com/the-year-of-the-poet

The Year of the Poet VIII
May 2021

Featured Global Poets
Paramita Mukherjee Mullick * Rose Zerguine
Jaydeep Sarangi * Bismay Mohanty

Diego Rivera

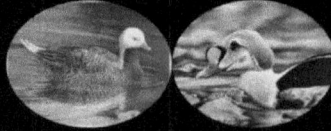

Poetry . . . Ekphrasticly Speaking
The Poetry Posse 2021
Gail Weston Shazor * Albert Carasso * Hülya N. Yılmaz
Jackie Davis Allen * Caroline Nazareno * Eliza Segiet
Alicja Maria Kuberska * Teresa E. Gallion * Joe Paire
Kimberly Burnham * Shareef Abdur – Rasheed
Ashok K. Bhargava * Elizabeth Castillo * Swapna Behera
Tezmin Ition Tsai * William S. Peters, Sr.

The Year of the Poet VIII
June 2021

Featured Global Poets
Alonzo "zO" Gross * Lali Tsipi Michaeli
Tareq al Karmy * Tirthendu Ganguly

Rayen Kang

Poetry . . . Ekphrasticly Speaking
The Poetry Posse 2021
Gail Weston Shazor * Albert Carasso * Hülya N. Yılmaz
Jackie Davis Allen * Caroline Nazareno * Eliza Segiet
Alicja Maria Kuberska * Teresa E. Gallion * Joe Paire
Kimberly Burnham * Shareef Abdur – Rasheed
Ashok K. Bhargava * Elizabeth Castillo * Swapna Behera
Tezmin Ition Tsai * William S. Peters, Sr.

The Year of the Poet VIII
July 2021

Featured Global Poets
Iram Jaan * Vesna Mundishevska-Veljanovska
Ngozi Olivia Osuoha * Lan Qyqalla

Goncalao Mabunda

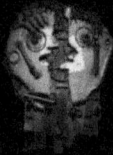

Poetry . . . Ekphrasticly Speaking
The Poetry Posse 2021
Gail Weston Shazor * Albert Carasso * Hülya N. Yılmaz
Jackie Davis Allen * Caroline Nazareno * Eliza Segiet
Alicja Maria Kuberska * Teresa E. Gallion * Joe Paire
Kimberly Burnham * Shareef Abdur – Rasheed
Ashok K. Bhargava * Elizabeth Castillo * Swapna Behera
Tezmin Ition Tsai * William S. Peters, Sr.

The Year of the Poet VIII
August 2021

Featured Global Poets
Caroline Laurent Turunc * Kamal Dhungana
Pankhuri Sinha * Paramita Mukherjee Mullick

Mundara Koorang

Poetry . . . Ekphrasticly Speaking
The Poetry Posse 2021
Gail Weston Shazor * Albert Carasso * Hülya N. Yılmaz
Jackie Davis Allen * Caroline Nazareno * Eliza Segiet
Alicja Maria Kuberska * Teresa E. Gallion * Joe Paire
Kimberly Burnham * Shareef Abdur – Rasheed
Ashok K. Bhargava * Elizabeth Castillo * Swapna Behera
Tezmin Ition Tsai * William S. Peters, Sr.

Now Available
www.innerchildpress.com/the-year-of-the-poet

The Year of the Poet VIII
September 2021
Featured Global Poets
Monsif Beroual * Sandesh Ghimire
Bhattila Poudel * Pavol Janik

Heather Jansch

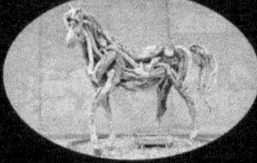

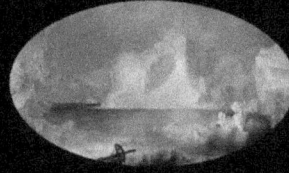

Poetry . . . Ekphrasticly Speaking

The Poetry Posse 2021

Gail Weston Shazor * Albert Carasco * Hülya N. Yılmaz
Jackie Davis Allen * Caroline Nazareno * Eliza Segiet
Alicja Maria Kuberska * Teresa E. Gallion * Joe Paire
Kimberly Burnham * Shareef Abdur – Rasheed
Ashok K. Bhargava * Elizabeth Castillo * Swapna Behera
Tezmin Ition Tsai * William S. Peters, Sr.

The Year of the Poet VIII
October 2021
Featured Global Poets
C. E. Shy * Baswala Ganguly
Suranjit Gain * Hasiba Hilal

Dale Lamphere

Poetry . . . Ekphrasticly Speaking

The Poetry Posse 2021

Gail Weston Shazor * Albert Carasco * Hülya N. Yılmaz
Jackie Davis Allen * Caroline Nazareno * Eliza Segiet
Alicja Maria Kuberska * Teresa E. Gallion * Joe Paire
Kimberly Burnham * Shareef Abdur – Rasheed
Ashok K. Bhargava * Elizabeth Castillo * Swapna Behera
Tezmin Ition Tsai * William S. Peters, Sr.

The Year of the Poet VIII
November 2021
Featured Global Poets
Errol D. Bean * Ibrahim Honjo
Tanja Ajtic * Rajashree Mohapatra

Andy Goldsworthy

Poetry . . . Ekphrasticly Speaking

The Poetry Posse 2021

Gail Weston Shazor * Albert Carasco * Hülya N. Yılmaz
Jackie Davis Allen * Caroline Nazareno * Eliza Segiet
Alicja Maria Kuberska * Teresa E. Gallion * Joe Paire
Kimberly Burnham * Shareef Abdur – Rasheed
Ashok K. Bhargava * Elizabeth Castillo * Swapna Behera
Tezmin Ition Tsai * William S. Peters, Sr.

The Year of the Poet VIII
December 2021
Featured Global Poets
Orbinda Ganga * Fadairo Tesleem
Anthony Arnold * Iyad Shamasnah

Fredric Edwin Church

Poetry . . . Ekphrasticly Speaking

The Poetry Posse 2021

Gail Weston Shazor * Albert Carasco * Hülya N. Yılmaz
Jackie Davis Allen * Caroline Nazareno * Eliza Segiet
Alicja Maria Kuberska * Teresa E. Gallion * Joe Paire
Kimberly Burnham * Shareef Abdur – Rasheed
Ashok K. Bhargava * Elizabeth Castillo * Swapna Behera
Tezmin Ition Tsai * William S. Peters, Sr.

Now Available

www.innerchildpress.com/the-year-of-the-poet

The Year of the Poet IX

January 2022

Featured Global Poets

**Ratan Ghosh * Christine Neil-Wright
Andrew Scott * Ashok Kumar**

Climate Change : The Ice Cap

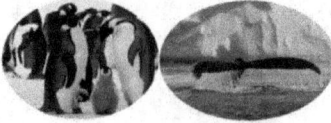

Poetry . . . Ekphrasticly Speaking

The Poetry Posse 2021

Gail Weston Shazor * Albert Carasso * Hülya N. Yılmaz
Jackie Davis Allen * Caroline Nazareno * Eliza Segiet
Alicja Maria Kuberska * Teresa E. Gallion * Joe Paire
Kimberly Burnham * Shareef Abdur – Rasheed
Ashok K. Bhargava * Elizabeth Castillo * Swapna Behera
Tezmin Ition Tsai * William S. Peters, Sr.

The Year of the Poet IX

February 2022

Featured Global Poets

Roza Boyanova * Ramón de Jesús Núñez Duval
Mammad Ismayil * Tarana Turan Rahimli

Climate Change and Mountains

Poetry . . . Ekphrasticly Speaking

The Poetry Posse 2021

Gail Weston Shazor * Albert Carasso * Hülya N. Yılmaz
Jackie Davis Allen * Caroline Nazareno * Eliza Segiet
Alicja Maria Kuberska * Teresa E. Gallion * Joe Paire
Kimberly Burnham * Shareef Abdur – Rasheed
Ashok K. Bhargava * Elizabeth Castillo * Swapna Behera
Tezmin Ition Tsai * William S. Peters, Sr.

The Year of the Poet IX

March 2022

Featured Global Poets

Dimitris P. Kraniotis * Marlene Pasini
Kennedy Ochieng * Swayam Prashant

Climate Change and Space Debris

Poetry . . . Ekphrasticly Speaking

The Poetry Posse 2021

Gail Weston Shazor * Albert Carasso * Hülya N. Yılmaz
Jackie Davis Allen * Caroline Nazareno * Eliza Segiet
Alicja Maria Kuberska * Teresa E. Gallion * Joe Paire
Kimberly Burnham * Shareef Abdur – Rasheed
Ashok K. Bhargava * Elizabeth Castillo * Swapna Behera
Tezmin Ition Tsai * William S. Peters, Sr.

The Year of the Poet IX

April 2022

Featured Global Poets

**Alonzo Gross * Dr. Debaprasanna Biswas
Monsif Beroual * Carol Aronoff**

Climate Change and Oceans

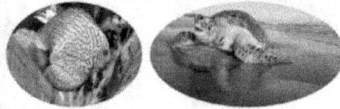

*Celebrating our 100th Edition *

Poetry . . . Ekphrasticly Speaking

The Poetry Posse 2021

Gail Weston Shazor * Albert Carasso * Hülya N. Yılmaz
Jackie Davis Allen * Caroline Nazareno * Eliza Segiet
Alicja Maria Kuberska * Teresa E. Gallion * Joe Paire
Kimberly Burnham * Shareef Abdur – Rasheed
Ashok K. Bhargava * Elizabeth Castillo * Swapna Behera
Tezmin Ition Tsai * William S. Peters, Sr.

Now Available

www.innerchildpress.com/the-year-of-the-poet

The Year of the Poet IX
May 2022

Featured Global Poets
Ndaba Sibanda * Smrutiranjan Mohanty
Ajanta Paul * Monalisa Dash Dwibedy

Climate Change and Birds

Poetry . . . Ekphrasticly Speaking

The Poetry Posse 2021

Gail Weston Shazor * Albert Carasco * Hülya N. Yılmaz
Jackie Davis Allen * Caroline Nazareno * Eliza Segiet
Alicja Maria Kuberska * Teresa E. Gallion * Joe Paire
Kimberly Burnham * Shareef Abdur – Rasheed
Ashok K. Bhargava * Elizabeth Castillo * Swapna Behera
Tezmin Ition Tsai * William S. Peters, Sr.

The Year of the Poet IX
June 2022

Featured Global Poets
Yuan Changming * Azeezat Okuniola
Tanja Ajtić * Philip Chijioke Abonyi

Climate Change and Trees

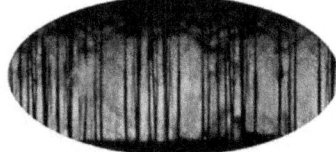

Poetry . . . Ekphrasticly Speaking

The Poetry Posse 2022

Gail Weston Shazor * Albert Carasco * Hülya N. Yılmaz
Jackie Davis Allen * Caroline Nazareno * Eliza Segiet
Alicja Maria Kuberska * Teresa E. Gallion * Joe Paire
Kimberly Burnham * Shareef Abdur – Rasheed
Ashok K. Bhargava * Elizabeth Castillo * Swapna Behera
Tezmin Ition Tsai * William S. Peters, Sr.

The Year of the Poet IX
July 2022

Featured Global Poets
Michelle Joan Barulich * Mili Das
Anna Ferriero * Ujjal Mandal

Climate Change and Animals

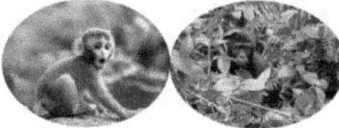

Poetry . . . Ekphrasticly Speaking

The Poetry Posse 2022

Gail Weston Shazor * Albert Carasco * Hülya N. Yılmaz
Jackie Davis Allen * Caroline Nazareno * Eliza Segiet
Alicja Maria Kuberska * Teresa E. Gallion * Joe Paire
Kimberly Burnham * Shareef Abdur – Rasheed
Ashok K. Bhargava * Elizabeth Castillo * Swapna Behera
Tezmin Ition Tsai * William S. Peters, Sr.

The Year of the Poet IX
August 2022

Featured Global Poets
Pankhuri Sinha * Abdulloh Abdumominov
Caroline Turunç * Tali Cohen Shabtai

Climate Change and Agriculture

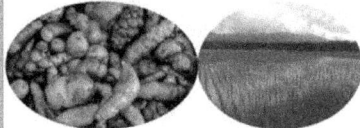

Poetry . . . Ekphrasticly Speaking

The Poetry Posse 2022

Gail Weston Shazor * Albert Carasco * Hülya N. Yılmaz
Jackie Davis Allen * Caroline Nazareno * Eliza Segiet
Alicja Maria Kuberska * Teresa E. Gallion * Joe Paire
Kimberly Burnham * Shareef Abdur – Rasheed
Ashok K. Bhargava * Elizabeth Castillo * Swapna Behera
Tezmin Ition Tsai * William S. Peters, Sr.

Now Available
www.innerchildpress.com/the-year-of-the-poet

The Year of the Poet IX
September 2022

Featured Global Poets

Ngozi Olivia Osuoha * Biswajit Mishra
Sylwia K. Malinowska * Sajid Hussein

Climate Change and Wind and Weather Patterns

Poetry ... Ekphrasticly Speaking

The Poetry Posse 2022

Gail Weston Shazor * Albert Carasrco * Hülya N. Yılmaz
Jackie Davis Allen * Caroline Nazareno * Eliza Segiet
Alicja Maria Kubanska * Teresa E. Gallion * Joe Paire
Kimberly Burnham * Shareef Abdur – Rasheed
Ashok K. Bhargava * Elizabeth Castillo * Swapna Behera
Tezmin Ition Tsai * William S. Peters, Sr.

The Year of the Poet IX
October 2022

Featured Global Poets

Andrew Kouroupos * Brenda Mohammed
Carthornia Kouroupos * Faleeha Hassan

Climate Change and Oil and Power

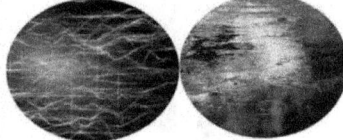

Poetry ... Ekphrasticly Speaking

The Poetry Posse 2022

Gail Weston Shazor * Albert Carasrco * Hülya N. Yılmaz
Jackie Davis Allen * Caroline Nazareno * Eliza Segiet
Alicja Maria Kubanska * Teresa E. Gallion * Joe Paire
Kimberly Burnham * Shareef Abdur – Rasheed
Ashok K. Bhargava * Elizabeth Castillo * Swapna Behera
Tezmin Ition Tsai * William S. Peters, Sr.

The Year of the Poet IX
November 2022

Featured Global Poets

Hema Ravi * Shafkat Aziz Hajam
Selma Kopic * Ibrahim Honjo

Climate Change : Time to Act

Poetry ... Ekphrasticly Speaking

The Poetry Posse 2022

Gail Weston Shazor * Albert Carasrco * Hülya N. Yılmaz
Jackie Davis Allen * Caroline Nazareno * Eliza Segiet
Alicja Maria Kubanska * Teresa E. Gallion * Joe Paire
Kimberly Burnham * Shareef Abdur – Rasheed
Ashok K. Bhargava * Elizabeth Castillo * Swapna Behera
Tezmin Ition Tsai * William S. Peters, Sr.

The Year of the Poet IX
December 2022

Featured Global Poets

Elarbi Abdelfattah * Lorraine Cragg
Neha Bhandarkar * Robert Gibbons

Climate Change Bees, Butterflies and Insect Life

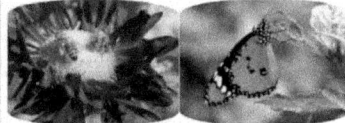

Poetry ... Ekphrasticly Speaking

The Poetry Posse 2022

Gail Weston Shazor * Albert Carasrco * Hülya N. Yılmaz
Jackie Davis Allen * Caroline Nazareno * Eliza Segiet
Alicja Maria Kubanska * Teresa E. Gallion * Joe Paire
Kimberly Burnham * Shareef Abdur – Rasheed
Ashok K. Bhargava * Elizabeth Castillo * Swapna Behera
Tezmin Ition Tsai * William S. Peters, Sr.

Now Available

www.innerchildpress.com/the-year-of-the-poet

The Year of the Poet X
January 2023

Featured Global Poets

JuNe Barefield * Swayam Prashant
Willow Rose * Shabbirhusein K Jamnagerwalla

Children : Difference Makers

Iqbal Masih

The Poetry Posse 2023

Gail Weston Shazor * Albert Carasco * Hülya N. Yılmaz
Jackie Davis Allen * Caroline Nazareno * Kimberly Burnham
Alicja Maria Kuberska * Teresa E. Gallion * Joe Paire
Michelle Joan Barulich * Shareef Abdur – Rasheed
Ashok K. Bhargava * Elizabeth Castillo * Swapna Behera
Tezmin Ition Tsai * Eliza Segiet * William S. Peters, Sr.

The Year of the Poet X
February 2023

Featured Global Poets

Christena Williams * Hilda Graciela Kraft
Francesco Favetta * Dr. H.C. Louise Hudon

Children : Difference Makers

Ruby Bridges

The Poetry Posse 2023

Gail Weston Shazor * Albert Carasco * Hülya N. Yılmaz
Jackie Davis Allen * Caroline Nazareno * Kimberly Burnham
Alicja Maria Kuberska * Teresa E. Gallion * Joe Paire
Michelle Joan Barulich * Shareef Abdur – Rasheed
Ashok K. Bhargava * Elizabeth Castillo * Swapna Behera
Tezmin Ition Tsai * Eliza Segiet * William S. Peters, Sr.

The Year of the Poet X
March 2023

Featured Global Poets

Clarena Martinez Turizo * Binod Dawadi
Til Kumari Sharma * Petrouchka Alexieva

Children : Difference Makers

Yo Yo Ma

The Poetry Posse 2023

Gail Weston Shazor * Albert Carasco * Hülya N. Yılmaz
Jackie Davis Allen * Caroline Nazareno * Kimberly Burnham
Alicja Maria Kuberska * Teresa E. Gallion * Joe Paire
Michelle Joan Barulich * Shareef Abdur – Rasheed
Ashok K. Bhargava * Elizabeth Castillo * Swapna Behera
Tezmin Ition Tsai * Eliza Segiet * William S. Peters, Sr.

The Year of the Poet X
April 2023

Featured Global Poets

Maxwanette A Poetess * Alonzo Gross
Türkan Ergör * Ibrahim Honjo

Children : Difference Makers

Claudette Colvin

The Poetry Posse 2023

Gail Weston Shazor * Albert Carasco * Hülya N. Yılmaz
Jackie Davis Allen * Caroline Nazareno * Kimberly Burnham
Alicja Maria Kuberska * Teresa E. Gallion * Joe Paire
Michelle Joan Barulich * Shareef Abdur – Rasheed
Ashok K. Bhargava * Elizabeth Castillo * Swapna Behera
Tezmin Ition Tsai * Eliza Segiet * William S. Peters, Sr.

Now Available
www.innerchildpress.com/the-year-of-the-poet

The Year of the Poet X
September 2023

Featured Global Poets
Eftichia Karpadeli * Chinh Nguyen
Nigar Agalarova * Carmela Cueva

Children : Difference Makers

~ Easton LaChappelle ~
The Poetry Posse 2023

Gail Weston Shazor * Albert Carasco * Hülya N. Yılmaz
Jackie Davis Allen * Caroline Nazareno * Kimberly Burnham
Alicja Maria Kuberska * Teresa E. Gallion * Joe Paire
Michelle Joan Barulich * Shareef Abdur - Rasheed
Ashok K. Bhargava * Elizabeth Castillo * Swapna Behera
Tezmin Ition Tsai * Eliza Segiet * William S. Peters, Sr.

The Year of the Poet X
October 2023

Featured Global Poets
CSP Shrivastava * Huniie Parker
Noreen Snyder * Ramkrishna Paul

Children : Difference Makers

~ Malala Yousafzai ~
The Poetry Posse 2023

Gail Weston Shazor * Albert Carasco * Hülya N. Yılmaz
Jackie Davis Allen * Caroline Nazareno * Kimberly Burnham
Alicja Maria Kuberska * Teresa E. Gallion * Joe Paire
Michelle Joan Barulich * Shareef Abdur - Rasheed
Ashok K. Bhargava * Elizabeth Castillo * Swapna Behera
Tezmin Ition Tsai * Eliza Segiet * William S. Peters, Sr.

The Year of the Poet X
November 2023

Featured Global Poets
Ibrahim Honjo * Balachandran Nair
Xanthi Hondrou-Hil * Francesco Favetta

Children : Difference Makers

~ Jean-Michel Basquiat ~
The Poetry Posse 2023

Gail Weston Shazor * Albert Carasco * Hülya N. Yılmaz
Jackie Davis Allen * Caroline Nazareno * Kimberly Burnham
Alicja Maria Kuberska * Teresa E. Gallion * Joe Paire
Michelle Joan Barulich * Shareef Abdur - Rasheed
Ashok K. Bhargava * Elizabeth Castillo * Swapna Behera
Tezmin Ition Tsai * Eliza Segiet * William S. Peters, Sr.

The Year of the Poet X
December 2023

Featured Global Poets
Caroline Laurent Turunc * Neha Bhandarkar
Shafkat Aziz Hajam * Elarbi Abdelfattah

Children : Difference Makers

~ Melati and Isabel Wijsen ~
The Poetry Posse 2023

Gail Weston Shazor * Albert Carasco * Hülya N. Yılmaz
Jackie Davis Allen * Caroline Nazareno * Kimberly Burnham
Alicja Maria Kuberska * Teresa E. Gallion * Joe Paire
Michelle Joan Barulich * Shareef Abdur - Rasheed
Ashok K. Bhargava * Elizabeth Castillo * Swapna Behera
Tezmin Ition Tsai * Eliza Segiet * William S. Peters, Sr.

Now Available

www.innerchildpress.com/the-year-of-the-poet

The Year of the Poet XI
June 2024

Featured Global Poets

C. S. P Shrivastava * Maria Evelyn Quilla Soleta
Moulay Cherif Chebihi Hassani * Swayam Prashant

Renowned Poets

~ Langston Hughs ~
The Poetry Posse 2024

Gail Weston Shazor * Albert Carassco * Hülya N. Yılmaz
Jackie Davis Allen * Caroline Nazareno * Mutawaf Shaheed
Alicja Maria Kuberska * Teresa E. Gallion * Noreen Snyder
Michelle Joan Barulich * Shareef Abdur – Rasheed
Ashok K. Bhargava * Elizabeth Castillo * Swapna Behera
Tezmin Ition Tsai * Eliza Segiet * William S. Peters, Sr.

The Year of the Poet XI
May 2024

Featured Global Poets

Binod Dawadi * Petros Kyriakou Veloudas
Rajame Ahmad Kamal * Solomon C. Jatta

Renowned Poets

~ Makhanlal Chaturvedi ~
The Poetry Posse 2024

Gail Weston Shazor * Albert Carassco * Hülya N. Yılmaz
Jackie Davis Allen * Caroline Nazareno * Mutawaf Shaheed
Alicja Maria Kuberska * Teresa E. Gallion * Noreen Snyder
Michelle Joan Barulich * Shareef Abdur – Rasheed
Ashok K. Bhargava * Elizabeth Castillo * Swapna Behera
Tezmin Ition Tsai * Eliza Segiet * William S. Peters, Sr.

Now Available

www.innerchildpress.com/the-year-of-the-poet

and there is much, much more !

visit . . .

www.innerchildpress.com/antho
logies-sales-special.php

Also check out our Authors and
all the wonderful Books
Available at :

www.innerchildpress.com/autho
rs-pages

World Healing World Peace
2020

Poets for Humanity

Now Available

www.worldhealingworldpeacepoetry.com

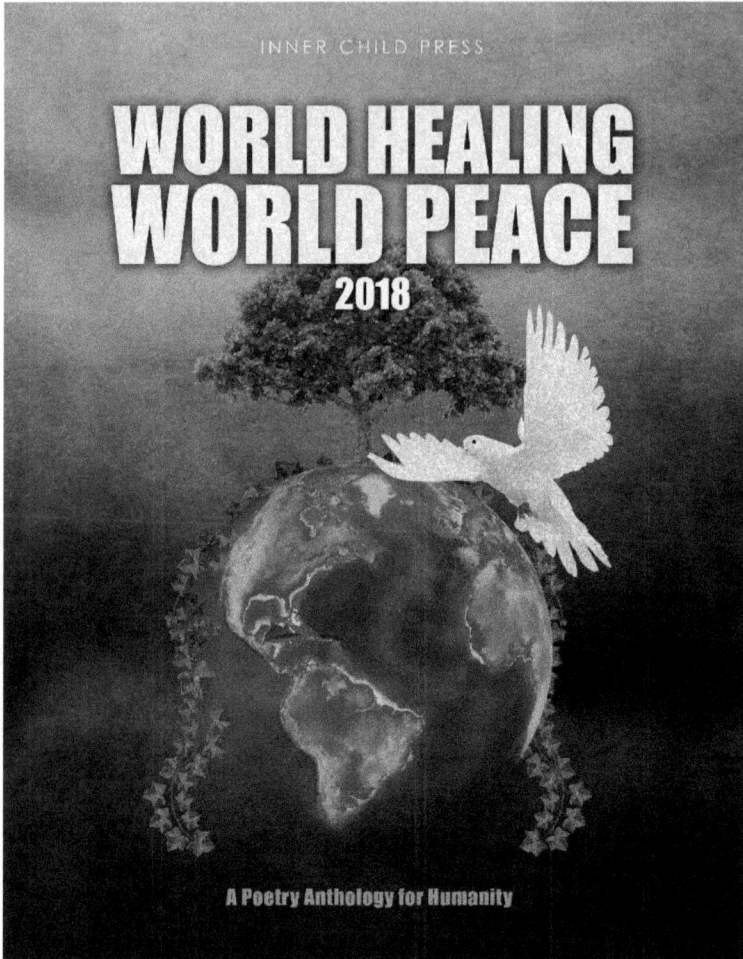

INNER CHILD PRESS

WORLD HEALING
WORLD PEACE
2018

A Poetry Anthology for Humanity

Now Available

www.worldhealingworldpeacepoetry.com

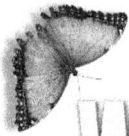

World Healing World Peace

I support

www.worldhealingworldpeacepoetry.com

World Healing World Peace

POEtRy

i am a believer !

World Healing
World Peace
2012, 2014, 2016, 2018, 2020, 2022

Now Available

www.worldhealingworldpeacepoetry.com

Inner Child Press International

building bridges of cultural understanding

Meet our Cultural Ambassadors

Fahredin Shehu
Director of Cultural

Faleha Hassan
Iraq – USA

Elizabeth E. Castillo
Philippines

Antoinette Coleman
Chicago
Midwest USA

Ananda Nepall
Nepal - Tibet
Northern India

Kimberly Burnham
Pacific Northwest
USA

Alicja Kuberska
Poland
Eastern Europe

Swapna Behera
India
Southeast Asia

Kolade O. Freedom
Nigeria
West Africa

Monsif Beroual
Morocco
Northern Africa

Ashok K. Bhargava
Canada

Tzemin Ition Tsai
Republic of China
Greater China

Alicia M. Ramirez
Mexico
Central America

Christena AV Williams
Jamaica
Caribbean

Louise Hudon
Eastern Canada

Aziz Mountassir
Morocco
Northern Africa

Shareef Abdur-Rasheed
Southeastern USA

Laure Charazac
France
Western Europe

Mohammad Ikbal Harb
Lebanon
Middle East

Mohamed Abdel
Aziz Shmeis
Egypt
Middle East

Hilary Mainga
Kenya
Eastern Africa

Josephus R. Johnson
Liberia

Mennadi Farah
Algeria

www.innerchildpress.com

This Anthological Publication
is underwritten solely by

Inner Child Press International

Inner Child Press is a Publishing Company Founded and Operated by Writers. Our personal publishing experiences provides us an intimate understanding of the sometimes daunting challenges Writers, New and Seasoned may face in the Business of Publishing and Marketing their Creative "Written Work".

For more Information

Inner Child Press International

www.innerchildpress.com

'building bridges of cultural understanding'
202 Wiltree Court. State College, Pennsylvania 16801

www.innerchildpress.com

251

~ fini ~

www.ingramcontent.com/pod-product-compliance
Lightning Source LLC
La Vergne TN
LVHW051041080426
835508LV00019B/1636